D0119488

The Scottish Milk Marketing Board would
like to thank the following for supplying
accessories for photography —
Douglas Weir House Furnishings, Glasgow
MacGregor & Co. (Glass & China) Ltd., Edinburgh
Ceramic Tiles — Gallery 2000, Glasgow.

ISBN 0 903438 06 2

Design and Photography Davis Design Studios, Glasgow
Printed by Cambus Litho, East Kilbride

Published by
The Scottish Milk Marketing Board
Underwood Road, Paisley

Contents

Eating for Goodness Sake

Whether you enjoy cooking or just delight in good food, it is hoped that you will find many dishes in this book which will tempt your palate.

With this thought in mind the Home Economists of The Scottish Milk Marketing Board have selected recipes which are quite quick to make and which have given them a lot of pleasure.

Scotland is extremely fortunate in having a very high quality of basic foods. Meat, fish and poultry are of a high standard and there is a plentiful supply of fruit, vegetables, eggs and dairy produce.

With these foods available, it it not only tempting, but also not too difficult to produce tasty and delicious dishes with relatively little effort.

The first section deals in detail with the different types of dairy produce available and gives advice on storage and use. The main part of the book contains recipes for every occasion. The last section consists of recipes using basic skills in a clearly photographed step-by-step form, particularly suitable for the inexperienced cook.

Metric measures and oven temperatures have been used throughout the book and imperial equivalents are given. Conversions are based on 25 g = 1 oz., 560 ml = 1 pint, 2.5 cm = 1 inch, in accordance with Standard British Practice. With larger amounts, quantities have been rounded up or down and have been appropriately balanced.

Milk

A lot of the food we eat nowadays is processed and fortified, dehydrated then reconstituted, frozen then thawed. Many foods contain artificial preservatives, flavourings and colourings. When you buy a pint of milk, however, you can be confident that it is 100% natural goodness.
Milk is a vital part of our diet from birth to retirement and has an important nutritional role at every stage throughout our lives.

It is the only food which contains all the nutrients necessary to maintain life and promote body growth. Proteins, fat, carbohydrates, mineral elements and vitamins are present in milk in well balanced proportions.

NUTRITIONAL VALUE OF A PINT OF MILK

	nutrients per pint
Energy	380 kcal 1,592 kJ
Protein	19.3 g
Fat	22.2 g
Carbohydrate	27.5 g
Calcium	702 mg
Iron	0.6 mg
Vitamin A (retinol equivalent)	230 μg
Thiamin	0.23 mg
Riboflavin	1.11 mg
Nicotinic acid equivalent	5.3 mg
Vitamin C	9 mg
Vitamin D	0.13 μg

TAKEN FROM "MANUAL OF NUTRITION" EIGHTH EDITION PUBLISHED BY HER MAJESTY'S STATIONERY OFFICE

There are many different types of milk on the market. In Scotland the majority is pasteurised with an average fat content of 3.8%. A knowledge of the different types available will help you to make the most suitable choice for your family.

PASTEURISED
SILVER TOP
Milk which has been heated to 72°C (161°F) for at least 15 seconds, then rapidly cooled to not more than 10°C (50°F). Pasteurised milk can be kept in a cool place for 1-2 days or 3-4 days in a refrigerator. You can see the cream line in this milk and it is ideal for everyday use, for drinking by the glass, for cooking, for hot drinks and on cereals.

HOMOGENIZED
RED TOP
This is pasteurised milk which by means of forcing milk through a very fine aperture, breaks down the fat globules and disperses them evenly through the milk. This type of milk is mostly supplied in bulk form to the catering trade in 13.6 or 22.7 litre (3 or 5 gallon) packs. It is cooled in a refrigerated dispenser and is generally found in cafes, restaurants, hospitals and canteens.

CHANNEL ISLANDS
GOLD TOP
Channel Islands milk must contain 4% butterfat and comes from a cow of the Jersey, Guernsey or South Devon breeds. It is very creamy milk but is not retailed widely in Scotland.

STERILIZED
Homogenized milk is filled into bottles which are capped with a metal cap and then the milk is heated to a temperature of not less than 100°C (212°F) and held at this temperature for a sufficient period of time. There is little demand for this milk in Scotland.

LOW FAT FRESH
This is a relatively new type of milk available with a butterfat content between 1.5 and 1.8%. This milk must be clearly labelled.

SKIMMED MILK
This is milk with the butterfat removed. This leaves non fat solids.

U.H.T.
The ultra heat treatment of milk or "Longlife" as it is sometimes referred to, is the process of heating homogenized milk to not less than 132°C (270°F) for at least one second and then it is cooled quickly and packaged in foil lined containers. It will keep for at least 3 months without refrigeration and is ideal for camping, sailing and as a reserve in your store cupboard.

TAKING CARE OF MILK

It is important to put milk in a cool place as soon as you get it, ideally in a fridge, but if one is not available stand the bottle in a bowl of cold water in a cool place, cover with a clean wet muslin cloth allowing each end to dip into the water. When storing milk keep it in the bottle or carton in which you got it and if returning a jug of milk to the fridge, cover it to stop other flavours being transferred to it. Pasteurised milk does not "sour" in the same way as untreated milk and should not be used once it has gone off.

CHILDREN AND MILK

As milk contains so many nutrients especially important to a growing child, it is worthwhile considering the many different ways in which this can be included in the diet. Cereals and porridge, hot drinks, coffee, soup, rice and other milk puddings, flans, milk jelly and custard are some ways in which milk can be included in the diet. Some children don't like milk straight from the bottle, but as milk is such a valuable food, it is very important that all children have milk in some form or another. There are many ways of encouraging children to drink milk. Milk is available in different flavours either fresh or as Longlife (UHT) milk. Commercial flavourings and powders can be added to milk which change the flavour and colour, but not the nutritional value. These come in many different flavours and can be used at the desired strength. Hot milk drinks are also a good way of getting children to take milk and if a child is ill this is an excellent way to build up strength again.

MILK FOR THE INVALID AND THE CONVALESCENT

Milk is of great value in the diet of invalids and convalescents because of its high food value. A good way to aid recovery is to give the most nutritious and most easily digestible food so that the body can benefit with the least effort and milk is a good source of vitamins and calcium. Food should be very carefully cooked, portions should be small and the tray for the invalid should be fresh and neatly set. Dishes such as junket, milky soups and even small sponge cakes with a little cream will be both nourishing and tempting.

Fresh Dairy Cream

Everyone loves the pure natural taste of real dairy cream. Added to the simplest dish it transforms it into "something special". Fresh cream has been associated for a long time with strawberries and raspberries but there are so many ways in which you can use it to enhance your cookery skills.
There is a range of creams available now to suit every need and palate and the following list will help you to choose the one that suits your needs most. Cream is described according to its butterfat content and there is a legal minimum for each type.

Half cream	12% butterfat
Pouring or Single cream	18% butterfat
Whipping cream	35% butterfat
Double cream	48% butterfat

USES FOR CREAMS

SINGLE CREAM

Single cream can be used in many ways — for coffee, porridge, cereals or fruit. Add a little to cream soups or pour it over either hot or cold sweets to make them mouthwatering. Single cream can also be used for salads, dressings, stews and sauces.

HALF CREAM

A light pouring cream ideal for coffee.

WHIPPING CREAM

This cream will whip and can be used for filling and decorating cakes and sweets. It can also be used in its unwhipped form for all the uses of single cream.

DOUBLE CREAM

Double cream can be used for all the uses associated with whipping and pouring cream. Because of its higher fat content, it will whip more quickly than whipping cream and will form a denser cream which will retain its shape longer after piping or decorating.

SOURED CREAM

This is single cream which has had a culture added to it to give a piquant flavour and a thicker texture. It can be used for both sweet and savoury dishes.
If you have difficulty in obtaining soured cream make your own by adding a teaspoonful of lemon juice to a 140 ml (5 oz) carton of single cream.

LONGLIFE CREAM

Longlife or Ultra Heat Treated (UHT) cream comes in three types, single, whipping and double and can be used in place of its fresh counterparts. This cream has been heat treated to enable it to be kept in a store cupboard for up to 12 weeks. It is handy to have in an emergency as is UHT milk.

STORAGE OF FRESH CREAM

Fresh cream should be kept in its original container as this has been sterilised. Keep it cool and covered, preferably in a refrigerator. Store away from strong flavoured foods.

How to whip cream for the best results. The cream, whisk and bowl should be really cold. The equipment can be placed in a refrigerator before use. The cream should be whipped quickly at first with a fork, balloon whisk or, rotary whisk. When it begins to thicken and take on a matt finish, beat more slowly until it stands in peaks. An electric mixer is not recommended as it is difficult not to overbeat cream when using one.

Butter

It takes the cream from about 11 litres (20 pts) of milk to make 500 g (1 lb 2 ozs) butter. The cream from the milk is churned into butter and a little salt is added to bring out the flavour and to help preserve the butter. Butter, like milk, is affected by light and should be stored in a cool dark place. There is nothing to touch the flavour of butter either as a spread or in cooking. A knob of butter when grilling steaks or in vegetables just before serving adds a lot in flavour and palatability. In the baking of rich fruit cakes and shortbread, butter is a must.

CLAYMORE
Orkney
FULL FAT HARD CHEESE
1 lb NET
CLAYMORE
Orkney Smoked
FULL FAT HARD CHEESE
1 lb NET
(454 grams)
PRODUCED & PACKED AT CLAYMORE CREAMERY·KIRKWALL·BY THE NORTH OF SCOTLAND MILK MARKETING BOARD
HOWGATE
MADE IN SCOTLAND
HOWGATE
FULL FAT SOFT CHEESE
Lothian
MADE IN SCOTLAND
FRESH NATURAL CHEESE
HIGHLAND CROWDIE
FRESH NATURAL CHEESE
CROWDIE AND CREAM
CABOC
THE DOUBLE CREAM CHEESE
ROLLED IN OATMEAL
CLAYMORE
CROWDIE
SCOTTISH ISLAND CHEESE
MADE WITH FULL CREAM PASTEURIZED MILK
ISLAY
DUNLOP CHEESE
NET WEIGHT 454g 1lb
ISLAY CREAMERY CO. LTD
ISLE OF ISLAY, SCOTLAND
CLAYMORE
CROWDIE
GALIC CHEESE
ROLLED IN
FLAKED OATS & NUTS
GALIC

Scottish Cheese

Scotland's climate provides ideal conditions for the lush grassland on which our dairy herds graze. From these herds comes the milk which goes into the making of Scottish cheese.

The tradition of cheesemaking in Scotland stretches back through the centuries. The old recipes and skills of the farmhouse have been adapted by our modern cheesemakers to make some of Britain's finest cheeses.

Scottish cheddars mild or mature, white or coloured, are established favourites all over the world and are famous for their high quality. Almost as well known is Dunlop cheese, a distinctive Scottish hard cheese originally made in the village of Dunlop in Ayrshire and now made on the Islands of Orkney, Arran and Islay. Dunlops are available as individual small cheeses weighing between 450g and 1kg (1 lb and 2¼ lbs) each.

The mainland of Scotland provides a very interesting selection of soft cheeses to tempt the palate. Some of these come from the Highlands. Caboc, a great favourite, is a rich double cream cheese rolled in pinhead oatmeal. Hramsa cheese is a soft cream cheese made with wild garlic and herbs which gives it a delicate, fresh taste. Galic is made from Hramsa cheese which is rolled in chopped nuts and is particularly delicious.

From the Lowlands come Pentland and Lothian, cheeses in the style of Brie and Camembert. From the same area comes a peat smoked soft cheese with a flavour which will appeal to admirers of smoked cheese. There is also in that area a cream cheese rolled in crushed peppercorns.

Cottage cheese is now widely popular and Scotland has many varieties either plain or with a varied selection of additions e.g. pineapple, chives, garlic or peppers.

A variety of Scottish cheese unique to Scotland is Crowdie. This is a traditional Highland cheese in the cottage cheese style made from skimmed milk and with a smoother texture. In one variation cream is added. Ideally, Crowdie should be eaten with oatcakes and Scottish butter.

Yogurt

Yogurt is now a very popular food and it is relatively easy to make at home. It can be made in a yogurt maker, in a vacuum flask or in a warm place such as an airing cupboard. If you haven't made it before, you will soon find the spot with the right conditions in your own home. There are many variations which you can make once you have the basic recipe ready.

HOME MADE SOFT YOGURT

560 ml (1 pint) pasteurised milk
1 teaspoon sugar (if further sweetening e.g. jam or honey is not used)
1 × 125g (5 oz) carton natural yogurt.

1. Warm the milk to blood heat (36°C, 98°F).
2. Remove from heat and stir in sugar.
3. Gently whisk in yogurt with a wire whisk or a fork.
4. Transfer to a bowl and cover.
5. Leave in a warm place or in vacuum flask for 8-12 hours, or until set.
6. If cold yogurt is preferred refrigerate after setting.

YIELD

Approximately ¾ litre (1¼ pints).
Once the yogurt has set it is ready for use, either as it is or with the addition of fruit or flavouring.
For firmer yogurt use UHT milk.
For low fat yogurt use skimmed milk with 1 dessertspoon instant milk powder added when warm.
For flavoured yogurt add either a fruit flavour or jam to add a touch of colour to the yogurt. The addition of a dessertspoon of honey makes a delicious yogurt. For fruit yogurt add small pieces of fresh, canned or thawed frozen fruit.
Interesting combinations can be made — chocolate and mint or coffee and walnut. You can add the flavouring before or after the yogurt is made. If you add the flavouring after the yogurt is made every member of the family can have his or her favourite flavour.

Flavouring	Amount used for (1 litre or 2 pints) of yogurt	Amount used for (125 ml or ¼ pint) of yogurt
Fruit — canned	1 small can	1 tablespoon
Fruit — fresh e.g. — strawberries	150 g (6 oz)	½ pear or ½ apple
Fruit — frozen (thawed)	150 g (6 oz)	1 tablespoon
Fruit juices from canned fruit if liked, or blackcurrant or orange juice	3-4 tablespoons	1 dessertspoon
Milk shake flavourings, coffee or cocoa powder	2-3 tablespoons (blended)	2-3 teaspoons (blended)
Essences	1-2 teaspoons	a few drops
Nuts	to taste	to taste
Sweetener (if wanted)		
Sugar	2 tablespoons	1 teaspoon
Saccharin	8 tablets	1 tablet
Honey	as sugar (use only after yogurt is made)	
Syrup	as sugar (use only after yogurt is made)	

Freezing of Dairy Produce

Freezing is a good way of preserving food but dairy produce is usually readily available all the year round and it is best to use it fresh. If, however, for any reason you have more than you can use, some dairy produce can be frozen. Produce which does not freeze well can be made up into sauces or sweets and then frozen.

Here is some information and hints on freezing dairy produce.

Milk Homogenized milk can be frozen for about a month in a plastic container. Do not freeze in a bottle. If you have any other type of milk that you can't use up, make it up into a dish which will freeze.

Cream Single cream does not freeze well but whipping and double cream will freeze, the best results are achieved by whipping lightly and if for a sweet dish, add a little sugar. If you have a small amount of whipped cream left, it can be piped in rosettes, frozen on trays then stored in a box. They can then be used as required.

Cheese Cheddar cheese tends to crumble when thawed, it is best to grate cheddar first then freeze. Soft cheeses tend to develop a stronger flavour.

Butter Butter freezes very well, especially if double wrapped in one layer of greaseproof and one layer of foil wrapping.

Yogurt Fruit yogurt freezes for about three months. If it separates slightly on thawing, stir well. Set yogurts do not freeze very successfully.

Recipes

Soups and Starters

Prawn Chowder

Ingredients

1 large onion, chopped
100g (4 oz) streaky bacon rashers, chopped
15g ($\frac{1}{2}$ oz) Scottish butter
450g(1 lb) potatoes
140ml ($\frac{1}{4}$ pt) ham stock
150g (6 oz) frozen prawns
560ml (1 pt) milk
75g (3 oz) Scottish cheddar cheese, grated
Seasoning

Number of servings: 4

Method

1. Melt butter and fry onion and bacon for several minutes.
2. Dice potatoes and put into saucepan with onion and bacon. Add stock and season.
3. Bring to the boil, cover and simmer gently for 10-15 minutes (or until potatoes are just cooked).
4. Add prawns and milk and reheat.
5. Remove from heat and stir in cheese. Serve immediately.

Deeside Regal

Ingredients

100g (4 oz) smoked salmon
16 asparagus spears (fresh or tinned)
140ml ($\frac{1}{4}$ pint) double cream
Seasoning
Triangles of brown bread
Scottish butter

Number of servings: 4

Method

1. Roll two asparagus spears in each piece of thinly sliced smoked salmon.
2. Place two rolls on each serving plate.
3. Whip cream to thick pouring consistency, season and pour over salmon rolls.
4. Serve with triangles of buttered brown bread and garnish with a lemon wedge.

Fruity Cheese Cocktails

Ingredients

2 oranges
1 grapefruit
100g (4 oz) Scottish cheddar cheese, grated
Dressing: 3 tablespoons lemon juice
2 tablespoons mayonnaise
2 tablespoons milk
A little paprika pepper
Seasoning

Number of servings: 4

Method

1. Peel oranges and grapefruit and cut into segments.
2. Arrange fruit in individual dishes, and sprinkle with grated cheese.
3. To make dressing, combine the lemon juice, mayonnaise, seasonings and milk together. Mix well.
4. Spoon dressing over fruit and cheese and sprinkle with a little paprika pepper.

Chilled Cucumber Soup

Ingredients

$\frac{1}{2}$ medium sized cucumber
2 × 125g (5 oz) cartons natural yogurt
1 × 175g (7oz) tin sweetcorn and peppers, drained
2 tablespoons cider vinegar
280ml ($\frac{1}{2}$ pt) chilled milk
Seasoning

Number of servings: 4

Method

1. Coarsely grate cucumber and add to yogurt together with sweetcorn and peppers. Add vinegar and seasoning.
2. Chill thoroughly.

Before serving, add the chilled milk and about 12 ice cubes.

Herb Potted Cheese

Ingredients
100-150g (4-6 oz) Scottish cheddar cheese, coarsely grated
50g (2 oz) Scottish butter
½ teaspoon salt
Freshly ground pepper
1 teaspoon dried mixed herbs
4 tablespoons sherry
Pinch dried mustard

Method

1. Mix cheese into softened butter, add seasoning, mustard and herbs, then beat in the sherry.
2. Press into a small earthenware dish.
3. Place a piece of waxed paper on the surface of the cheese, cover the dish with a lid or foil and keep in a cool place for several hours before serving with hot toast or melba toast.

French Onion Soup

Ingredients
2 large onions
50g (2 oz) Scottish butter
840ml (1½ pints) beef stock
1 glass white wine
Seasoning
Toasted cheese cubes or croûtons

Number of servings: 4

Method

1. Chop the onions and fry gently in butter until golden brown in colour — about 15 minutes. Season.
2. Add beef stock, bring to the boil then simmer for 45 minutes, season and add wine.
3. Serve garnished with toasted cheese cubes or croûtons.

Avocado Savoury

Ingredients
2 avocado pears
A little lemon juice
50g (2 oz) cottage cheese
50g (2 oz) tuna fish
2 tablespoons double cream
Seasoning

Number of servings: 4

Method

1. Cut pears in half and remove stones.
2. Remove flesh, cut roughly and add a little lemon juice to avoid discolouration.
3. Add cottage cheese, drained tuna fish and cream and mix well. Season.
4. Pile mixture into pear shells and garnish with a lemon twist.

Spaghetti Special

Ingredients
150g (6 oz) spaghetti
140ml ($\frac{1}{4}$ pint) single cream
1 teaspoon mixed herbs
1 clove finely chopped garlic
Seasoning
100g (4 oz) Scottish cheddar cheese, finely grated
$\frac{1}{2}$ green pepper
$\frac{1}{2}$ red pepper

Number of servings: 4

Method

1. Cook spaghetti in boiling salted water until tender (about 20 minutes). Drain well.
2. Gently heat the cream in a pan. Add seasoning, mixed herbs and garlic.
3. Toss cooked spaghetti in cream and serve sprinkled liberally with finely grated cheese. Garnish with rings of red and green pepper.

Lettuce Soup

Ingredients
225g (8 oz) lettuce leaves, approx. 2 lettuce
1 onion, chopped
40g (1 ½ oz) Scottish butter
420ml (¾ pint) chicken stock
Pinch caster sugar
Pinch grated nutmeg
Seasoning
420ml (¾ pint) milk
2 egg yolks
2 tablespoons single cream
Croûtons for garnish

Number of servings: 4-6

Method

1. Melt the butter in a saucepan and fry the onion until soft. Chop lettuce leaves and add to pan.
2. Pour the stock over the onions and lettuce and bring to the boil. Add caster sugar, nutmeg and seasoning.
3. Allow the soup to cool slightly before liquidising or rubbing through a sieve. Add the milk and reheat gently, simmer for 5 minutes.
4. Lightly beat together the egg yolks and cream. Spoon a little of the hot, but not boiling soup into this and blend thoroughly.
5. Pour the egg mixture into the soup and heat through gently. Do not boil the soup or the eggs will curdle.
6. Just before serving garnish with croûtons.

Crunchy Creamed Mushrooms

Ingredients
340g (12 oz) button mushrooms
50g (2 oz) Scottish butter
15g (½ oz) flour
140ml (¼ pt) double cream
Seasoning
1 clove garlic, finely chopped (optional)

Topping
50g (2 oz) Scottish cheddar cheese, grated
25g (1 oz) breadcrumbs
25g (1 oz) Scottish butter

Number of servings: 4

Method

1. Wash mushrooms and trim stalks if necessary.
2. Melt butter in pan, add mushrooms and chopped garlic, cook gently for a few minutes. Add flour to absorb excess moisture then add cream, stirring all the time.
3. Season and divide into 4 individual dishes.
4. For the topping, melt butter and add breadcrumbs and cheese. Divide topping between dishes.
5. Place under grill until topping is crisp.

Corn-on-the-Cob

Ingredients

4 cobs of corn
Slices flavoured butter

Parsley butter:	**100g (4 oz) Scottish butter, 15g ($\frac{1}{2}$ oz) chopped parsley, juice $\frac{1}{2}$ lemon, pinch cayenne pepper.**
Mustard butter:	**100g (4 oz) Scottish butter, 1 teaspoon mustard, juice $\frac{1}{2}$ lemon, seasoning.**
Pepper butter:	**100g (4 oz) Scottish butter, salt and freshly ground black pepper.**
Devilled butter:	**100g (4 oz) Scottish butter, $\frac{1}{2}$ teaspoon curry powder, $\frac{1}{2}$ teaspoon paprika pepper, juice $\frac{1}{2}$ lemon, pinch cayenne pepper.**
Shrimp butter	**100g (4 oz) Scottish butter, 100g (4 oz) cooked and puréed shrimps, juice $\frac{1}{2}$ lemon, seasoning.**

Number of servings: 4

Method

1. Flavoured butter to be served with the cobs, should be made well in advance so that it can be chilled. Cream the butter in a bowl until smooth. Add flavour ingredients and blend well with butter. Shape the butter into an oblong roll, wrap in greaseproof paper and chill in refrigerator until required.
2. Remove the husks and silky threads from the cobs. Cook the cobs in boiling water for 5-10 minutes. Drain.
3. Serve the cobs immediately with the butter cut into thick slices. Use corn on the cob holders, small skewers, strong toothpicks or cocktail sticks to hold the cobs at each end.

Salmon Mousse

Ingredients

3 level teaspoons gelatine
140ml ($\frac{1}{4}$ pint) hot water
140ml ($\frac{1}{4}$ pint) single cream
2 eggs, separated
$\frac{1}{2}$ teaspoon salt
1 tablespoon lemon juice
1 dessertspoon horseradish sauce
200g (7 oz) tin red salmon, drained and finely mashed
4 slices of lemon

Number of servings: 4

Method

1. Put gelatine and hot water in bowl. Stir until dissolved, over a pan of boiling water. Leave until lukewarm.
2. Add cream to beaten egg yolks. Combine with dissolved gelatine and stir in salt and lemon juice.
3. When cold and just beginning to thicken, stir in mashed salmon and horseradish sauce.

4. Beat egg whites to a stiff snow and gently fold into salmon mixture.
5. Pour into 4 ramekin dishes and chill until firm.
6. Just before serving garnish with a lemon twist.

Cheese & Tomato Soup

Ingredients
25g (1 oz) Scottish butter
1 small onion, finely chopped
25g (1 oz) plain flour
140ml ($\frac{1}{4}$ pint) chicken stock
560ml (1 pint) milk
100g (4 oz) tomatoes, skinned and chopped
150g (6 oz) Scottish cheddar cheese, finely grated
Seasoning

Number of servings: 4

Method

1. Melt butter in saucepan, add onion and fry gently. Add flour and cook for 1-2 minutes
2. Gradually blend in stock and milk. Cook, stirring until soup comes to the boil and thickens slightly.

3. Add tomatoes and season. Lower heat, cover pan and simmer for 10 minutes.
4. Remove from heat and add 125g (5 oz) cheese. Stir until cheese melts.
5. Serve sprinkled with remaining cheese.

Khura Cream

Ingredients
75g (3 oz) long grain rice
25g (1 oz) sultanas
50g (2 oz) single cream
1 teaspoon curry powder
50g (2 oz) prawns
70ml ($\frac{1}{8}$ pt) double cream } **Marie Rose Sauce**
1 tablespoon mayonnaise } **Marie Rose Sauce**
1 tablespoon tomato ketchup } **Marie Rose Sauce**
Seasoning } **Marie Rose Sauce**
1 lemon, sliced
Paprika pepper

Number of servings: 4

Method

1. Boil rice for 12 minutes in salted water; drain and cool.
2. Mix together rice, single cream, sultanas, curry powder and seasoning.
3. Divide into four individual dishes or wine glasses.
4. Place prawns on top of rice mixture.
5. Lightly whip double cream. Add mayonnaise and tomato ketchup. Season.
6. Pour sauce over prawns and sprinkle with a little paprika pepper.
7. Serve, garnished with a prawn and a slice of lemon.

N.B. This starter is also ideal to serve as a salad on a buffet table.

Avocado Marie Rose

Cut 2 ripe avocado pears in half, remove the stones then brush flesh with lemon juice to avoid discolouration. Divide 50g (2 oz) prawns between the halved pears. Make up Marie Rose Sauce (see Khura Cream recipe above) and pour over the prawns. Sprinkle with paprika pepper and garnish with lemon slices.

Prawn Cocktail

Place some shredded lettuce in the base of 4 glasses. Divide 225g (8 oz) prawns between the glasses. Make up a double quantity of Marie Rose Sauce (see Khura Cream recipe above) and pour over the prawns. Sprinkle with paprika pepper and garnish with lemon wedge and prawns. Serve with fingers of buttered brown bread.

Crunchy Shrimp Scallops

Ingredients
50g (2 oz) Scottish butter
225g (8 oz) shrimps, peeled
8 tablespoons double cream
Seasoning
$\frac{1}{2}$ packet potato crisps
450g (1 lb) potatoes, cooked and mashed with a little butter

Oven temperature:	180°C/350°F/No. 4
Position in oven:	Centre
Time in oven:	6-7 minutes
Number of servings:	4

Method

1. Lightly butter scallop type dishes. Place 50g (2 oz) of shrimps on each shell.
2. Cover each with two tablespoons of cream, and seasoning.
3. Finely crush the potato crisps and sprinkle over the shrimps.
4. Pipe potato round outside of dish and bake for 6-7 minutes.
5. Serve garnished with a few shrimps and a slice of lemon.

Farmhouse Favourite Soup

Ingredients
40g ($1\frac{1}{2}$oz) Scottish butter
40g ($1\frac{1}{2}$ oz) plain flour
420 ml ($\frac{3}{4}$ pt) milk
420 ml ($\frac{3}{4}$ pt) water
1 small carrot
1 small leek
Small piece of turnip
Seasoning

Number of servings: 4

Method
1. Grate carrot and turnip, chop leek finely and soak in water.
2. Blend flour and milk, add butter and stir until boiling. Season.
3. Add vegetables and liquid to sauce. Simmer for 25 minutes. Serve with hot crusty bread.

Cheesy Carrot Soup

Ingredients
1 large onion, chopped
2 large carrots, grated
40g ($1\frac{1}{2}$ oz) Scottish butter
40g ($1\frac{1}{2}$ oz) plain flour
420ml ($\frac{3}{4}$ pt) milk
420ml ($\frac{3}{4}$ pt) chicken stock
Seasoning
75g (3 oz) Scottish cheddar cheese, grated

Number of servings: 4

Method
1. Melt butter in a saucepan, add chopped onions and cook without colouring.
2. Stir in the flour and cook the roux for a few minutes.
3. Add the milk and chicken stock gradually, then stir in the grated carrots and seasoning. Bring to the boil, stirring all the time. Simmer for 15-20 minutes.
4. Serve sprinkled with grated cheese.

Delhi Crunch

Ingredients
225g (8 oz) cottage cheese
4 tablespoons mayonnaise
1 × 125g (5oz) carton natural yogurt
3-4 level teaspoons curry powder
3-4 tablespoons sultanas
Seasoning
$\frac{1}{2}$ head of celery

Number of servings: 4

Method
1. Beat cheese until smooth, together with mayonnaise and natural yogurt.
2. Stir in curry powder and season to taste.
3. Add 3 tablespoons sultanas and mix through.
4. Serve in celery stalks (cut into 8cm (3″) fingers) on a bed of lettuce with brown bread and butter.

N.B. This starter is also ideal to serve with savoury biscuits as a dip at a buffet or cocktail party.

Chicken Liver Pâté

Ingredients
100g (4 oz) lean bacon, thinly sliced
340g (12 oz) chicken livers
75g (3 oz) Scottish butter
2 tablespoons double cream
1 tablespoon sherry (optional)
Seasoning
1 slice of bacon to garnish

Number of servings: 4-6

Method

1. Wash and clean chicken livers and chop finely.
2. Melt ⅔ of butter in frying pan.
3. Add the chopped chicken livers and sliced bacon. Cook gently for about 10 minutes.
4. Add the sherry, cream and seasoning.
5. Place in a pâté dish and smooth off with a knife.
6. Decorate the top with slice of grilled bacon and pour remaining melted butter over top.
7. Put in fridge to cool for 2 hours before serving.

Cream of Mushroom Soup

Ingredients
100g (4 oz) mushrooms, sliced
40g (1½ oz) Scottish butter
50g (2 oz) plain flour
560ml (1 pint) milk
560ml (1 pint) chicken stock
50g (2 oz) double cream
Seasoning

Number of servings: 6

Method

1. Fry mushrooms in butter.
2. Add flour then gradually blend in the milk.
3. Stir over heat constantly until boiling.
4. Add stock and season. Simmer for five minutes.
5. If consistency is too thick, add extra milk.
6. To finish soup, add a swirl of cream just before serving.

Smoked Mackerel Pâté

Ingredients
225g (8 oz) smoked mackerel
50g (2 oz) Scottish butter
50g (2 oz) double cream, lightly whipped
1 teaspoon horseradish sauce
Lemon juice
Seasoning

Number of servings: 4

Method

1. Remove skin and break down smoked mackerel.
2. Cream butter in bowl. Add whipped cream, horseradish sauce, seasoning, squeeze of lemon juice and mackerel. Beat or liquidise mixture.
3. Press the mixture into one large dish or individual pâté dishes.
4. Garnish with lemon and parsley and serve with hot buttered toast, french bread or melba toast.

Cullen Skink

Ingredients
225g (8 oz) potato, diced
1 large onion, chopped
420ml ($\frac{3}{4}$ pt) milk
450g (1 lb) smoked haddock fillet
Seasoning
25g (1 oz) Scottish butter

Number of servings: 4

Method

1. Place potato, onion and milk in a saucepan. Cook gently for about 20 minutes until the vegetables are soft.
2. Cut the fish into chunks, add to the pan, cover and simmer for a further 20 minutes until cooked.
3. Stir in the butter and season, just before serving.

Cream of Sweetcorn Soup

Ingredients
1 x 275g (10 oz) tin creamed sweetcorn
100g (4 oz) frozen sweetcorn
225g (8 oz) potatoes, sliced
1 onion, finely chopped
25g (1 oz) Scottish butter
560ml (1 pt) milk
280ml ($\frac{1}{2}$ pt) chicken stock
Seasoning

Number of servings: 4

Method

1. Melt the butter in a pan, add potatoes and onion and cook until soft.
2. Add the milk, chicken stock, sweetcorn and seasoning. Bring to the boil, stirring all the time. Simmer for 15-20 mins.
3. Sieve soup or liquidise in a blender. Serve with croûtons.

Celery Soup

Ingredients
1 head or 450g (1 lb) celery, cut into pieces
225g (8 oz) potatoes, quartered
2 onions, sliced
25g (1 oz) Scottish butter
560ml (1 pt) ham stock
140ml ($\frac{1}{4}$ pt) milk
Pinch grated nutmeg
Seasoning
75g (3 oz) Scottish cheddar cheese, grated

Number of servings: 4

Method

1. Melt the butter in a saucepan, add celery and onion, cook gently without browning.
2. Add the potatoes to pan and pour in stock. Season and add nutmeg.
3. Bring to the boil and simmer until all are tender, about 15-20 minutes.
4. Allow the soup to cool slightly, then liquidise or sieve.
5. Add the milk, re-heat and adjust seasoning if necessary.
6. Serve hot sprinkled with grated cheese.

Nutty Peaches

Ingredients
4 peach halves
4 lettuce leaves
75g (3 oz) sweetcorn
25g (1 oz) salted peanuts
100g (4 oz) Scottish cheddar cheese, grated
1-2 tablespoons lightly whipped double cream
1-2 tablespoons salad cream
Seasoning
4 slices cucumber

Number of servings: 2

Method

1. Drain peach halves and place each on a lettuce leaf.
2. Mix sweetcorn, nuts and cheese and bind together with lightly whipped cream and salad cream. Season to taste.
3. Pile mixture on top of each peach and garnish with cucumber.

Fish and Shellfish

Salmon Quiche

Ingredients

Base:	**50g (2 oz) plain biscuits, crushed**
	50g (2 oz) Scottish butter
	25g (1 oz) Scottish cheddar cheese, grated
Filling:	**15g (½ oz) Scottish butter**
	25g (1 oz) onion, finely chopped
	15g (½ oz) flour
	2 tablespoons milk
	1 × 100g (3½ oz) tin salmon
	1 teaspoon lemon juice

Oven temperature: 180°C/350°F/No.4
Position in oven: Centre
Time in oven: 10 minutes
Number of servings: 4

Method

1. To make base: melt butter, add crushed biscuits, mix in grated cheese and press into an 18cm (7 inch) ovenproof dish.
2. Melt butter for filling, cook onion, add flour and cook for a few minutes. Add milk, juice from tin of salmon and lemon juice, and cook for a few minutes.
3. Add flaked salmon to mixture, pour into biscuit base. Place in a moderate oven for 10 minutes.
4. Decorate with slices of cucumber.

Cheddar Prawns

Ingredients

225g (8 oz) shelled prawns
25g (1 oz) Scottish butter
25g (1 oz) flour
280 ml (½ pint) milk
75g (3 oz) Scottish cheddar cheese, grated
Seasoning
150g (6 oz) long grain rice

Number of servings: 4

Method

1. To make up sauce, melt butter in pan. Stir in flour and cook for a few minutes. Remove from heat and gradually stir in milk.
2. Return to heat, bring to the boil stirring continuously.
3. Add cheese, prawns and seasoning. Heat thoroughly.
4. Boil rice in salted water for 12 minutes. Drain well.
5. Serve prawns on bed of rice.

N.B. A little wine can be substituted for some of the milk for special occasions.

Haddock Fluff

Ingredients

225g (8 oz) smoked haddock
50g (2 oz) white breadcrumbs
280ml (½ pint) milk
½ teaspoon lemon juice
1 teaspoon parsley, chopped
1 egg separated
Seasoning

Oven temperature: 200°C/400°F/No.6
Position in oven: Centre
Time in oven: 20 minutes
Number of servings: 4

Method

1. Cook fish in a little milk, then flake.
2. Heat remaining milk to blood temperature and whisk in egg yolk. Add fish, breadcrumbs, parsley, lemon juice and seasoning.
3. Whisk egg white until it holds soft peaks. Fold into fish mixture.

4. Place in a greased ½ litre (1 pint) dish and bake at 200°C/400°F/No.6 for 20 minutes or until set.

Hawaiian Haddock

Ingredients
225g (8 oz) smoked haddock, cooked and flaked
1 × 247g (8¾ oz) tin crushed pineapple
140ml (¼ pt) double cream
1 egg yolk
650g (1½ lb) mashed potato
Salt, pepper, pinch of nutmeg
50g (2 oz) Scottish cheddar cheese, grated

Oven temperature: 180°C/350°F/No. 4
Position in oven: Centre
Time in oven: 20 minutes
Number of servings: 4

Method
1. Place the pineapple in the base of an ovenproof dish.
2. Mix flaked fish into cream and place on top of pineapple.
3. Add egg yolk to potato and season with salt, pepper and nutmeg. Mix well.

4. Pipe or spread the potato round the dish. Sprinkle with grated cheese.
5. Place in a moderate oven for 20 minutes. Serve with a green salad.

Tomato & Tuna Hotpot

Ingredients
450g (1 lb) tomatoes, skinned and sliced
1 × 200g (7 oz) tin tuna fish, well drained
450g (1 lb) potatoes, boiled and sliced

Cheese Sauce
25g (1 oz) Scottish butter
25g (1 oz) flour
280ml (½ pint) milk
100g (4 oz) Scottish cheddar cheese, grated
Seasoning

Oven temperature: 200°C/400°F/No.6
Position in oven: Centre
Time in oven: 20 minutes
Number of servings: 4

Method
1. Arrange half the sliced tomatoes in the bottom of a 1 litre (2 pint) ovenproof dish. Spread the tuna fish over the tomatoes.

2. Place the rest of the tomatoes on the fish and top with slices of potato.
3. Cheese Sauce: Melt butter, add flour and cook for 1 minute. Remove from heat and stir milk in gradually. Return to heat and bring to boil stirring continuously. Add seasoning and 75g (3 oz) grated cheese. Stir until cheese has melted.
4. Pour the cheese sauce over the hotpot, sprinkle on remaining grated cheese and heat through in a fairly hot oven.

Seafood Pancakes

Ingredients

Batter: 100g (4oz) flour, 1 egg, pinch of salt, 280ml ($\frac{1}{2}$ pint) milk. Scottish butter for frying

Filling: 1 × 200g (7 oz) tin of tuna fish, drained

Sauce: 50g (2 oz) Scottish butter
140ml ($\frac{1}{4}$ pint) double cream
2 tablespoons dry sherry or white wine
Pinch of ground nutmeg
200g (7 oz) prawns
40g (1$\frac{1}{2}$ oz) flour
280ml ($\frac{1}{2}$ pint) milk
Seasoning
Pinch of paprika

Number of servings: 4

Method

1. Make batter using the flour, salt, egg and milk. (See Step by Step Cookery, page 120) Beat until smooth. Use this batter to make 8 pancakes.
2. Flake the tuna fish and divide between the pancakes. Roll up and place on a warmed serving dish and place in a warm oven to heat through.
3. For sauce, melt butter, stir in flour, cream, milk and sherry or white wine. Heat, stirring continuously until the sauce thickens. Season. Add nutmeg, paprika and prawns and heat through.
4. Pour sauce over pancakes and garnish with chopped parsley.

Crunchy Cod Casserole

Ingredients

225g (8 oz) cod
225g (8 oz) cooked potato, diced
2 hard boiled eggs, chopped
1 tablespoon leek, chopped
280 ml ($\frac{1}{2}$ pt) milk
25g (1 oz) Scottish butter
50g (2 oz) Scottish cheddar cheese, grated
Seasoning
25g (1oz) flour

Topping: 25g (1 oz) rolled oats
75g (3 oz) Scottish cheddar cheese, grated

Number of servings: 4

Method

1. Poach fish in a little of the measured milk. Drain liquid and flake fish.
2. Add remaining milk to liquid, then blend it with the flour. Add butter, bring sauce to the boil stirring constantly. Cook for 2 minutes. Season.
3. Mix cheese, potato, eggs and leek into sauce. Stir in flaked fish. Heat through.
4. Place mixture in a 1 litre (2 pint) ovenproof dish.
5. Make topping by mixing rolled oats and grated cheese together. Sprinkle over fish mixture. Place under hot grill until topping is crisp and golden brown.

Creamy Kedgeree

Ingredients

100g (4 oz) long grain rice
75g (3 oz) Scottish butter
140ml ($\frac{1}{4}$ pint) double cream
225g (8 oz) smoked haddock, cooked and flaked
2 hard boiled eggs, chopped
50g (2 oz) raisins
Seasoning
1 hard boiled egg, sliced for garnish

Number of servings: 4

Method

1. Boil rice for 12 minutes in salted water and drain.
2. Melt butter in pan, add cream.
3. Stir in cooked rice, fish, eggs and raisins and cook over a low heat for a few minutes.
4. Season and serve with sliced hard boiled egg.

Note — 140ml ($\frac{1}{4}$ pint) cheese sauce can be substituted for the 140ml ($\frac{1}{4}$ pint) cream to make a more economical dish.

Herbie Haddock

Ingredients

4 haddock fillets
25g (1 oz) Scottish butter
2 tablespoons breadcrumbs
$\frac{1}{4}$ teaspoon mixed herbs
4 tablespoons Scottish cheddar cheese, grated
Seasoning
Little milk

Oven temperature:	190°C/375°F/No.5
Position in oven:	Centre
Time in oven:	15-20 minutes
Number of servings:	4

Method

1. Wash fish, season and place in an ovenproof dish.
2. Melt butter. Add breadcrumbs, herbs and grated cheese, mix well.
3. Place some of the mixture on top of each fillet then pour a little milk round the fish.
4. Bake for 15-20 minutes. When cooked, brown under grill to crisp up topping.

Sole à la Crème

Ingredients

75g (3 oz) Scottish butter
4 fillets lemon sole
Juice of 1 lemon
140ml ($\frac{1}{4}$ pint) double cream
Seasoning

Number of servings: 4

Method

1. Melt butter in frying pan and gently fry sole with lemon juice added. When sole is cooked, remove from pan and keep warm.
2. Add cream to butter and lemon juice in which sole was cooked and bring to boil. Boil for 1-2 minutes until all ingredients are mixed together and begin to thicken.
3. Test for seasoning. Remove from heat immediately and pour over sole.

Prawn Curry

Ingredients

25g (1 oz) Scottish butter
1 large onion, chopped
1 garlic clove, crushed
½ teaspoon salt
½ teaspoon turmeric
1 teaspoon ground ginger
1 teaspoon chilli powder
1 × 396g (14 oz) tin tomatoes, drained
450g (1 lb) fresh prawns
1 teaspoon lemon juice
1 × 125g (5 oz) carton natural yogurt
150g (6 oz) long grain rice

Number of servings: 4

Method

1. Heat butter in a frying pan. Add the onion and garlic and fry for 5 minutes or until golden.
2. Stir in the spices and fry for 2-3 minutes. Add the tomatoes and cook for 10 minutes.
3. Add the prawns and cook gently for 10-15 minutes. Stir in the lemon juice and yogurt.
4. Serve on a bed of boiled rice.

Sweet and Savoury Sauces

Béchamel Sauce

Ingredients
1 small onion
Small piece of turnip
Small piece of carrot
1 bay leaf
280ml (½ pint) milk
25g (1 oz) Scottish butter
25g (1 oz) flour
Seasoning
2 tablespoons double cream

Number of servings: 4

Method
1. Simmer vegetables and bay leaf in milk for 15 minutes.
2. Strain milk and make up as for white sauce (see Step by Step Cookery, page 114)
3. Add cream just before serving.

Variations
Cucumber Sauce: Grate ½ cucumber and marinate in a mixture of tarragon vinegar, malt vinegar and water (1/3 each). Refrigerate for an hour. Drain well and add to 1 pint béchamel sauce. Excellent with poached salmon or mackerel.

Shrimp Sauce: 2 tablespoons of shelled chopped shrimps with 1 tablespoon of tomato purée to 1 pint béchamel sauce. Ideal for fish dishes.

Mornay Sauce: 2 egg yolks, 4 tablespoons double cream and 4 tablespoons finely grated Scottish cheddar cheese to 1 pint béchamel sauce. Reheat over a low heat. Do not boil.

Bread Sauce

Ingredients
1 onion
4 cloves
1 bayleaf
4 peppercorns
Pinch nutmeg
560ml (1 pint) milk
125g (5oz) fresh white breadcrumbs
25g (1 oz) Scottish butter
3 tablespoons single cream
Seasoning

Number of servings: 8

Method
1. Peel the onion and stud it with the cloves. Put the onion, bayleaf, peppercorns, nutmeg and milk in a saucepan.
2. Bring to the boil, then remove from heat, cover with a lid and leave to infuse for 15 minutes. Strain.
3. Combine hot milk, breadcrumbs, butter and cream. Season. Serve with chicken or turkey.

Hollandaise Sauce

Ingredients
3 egg yolks
1 tablespoon lemon juice
1 tablespoon water
125g (5 oz) Scottish butter, melted
Seasoning

Number of servings: 6

Method
1. Blend the egg yolks, lemon juice, water and seasoning together in a liquidiser.
2. Turn the blender to high speed and slowly add the melted butter. Liquidise for about 30 seconds until thick and fluffy.
3. Serve immediately or keep warm by standing the sauce over warm water.

Serve over cooked asparagus, broccoli or courgettes or with poached fish, egg or chicken dishes.

Yogurt Sauce

Ingredients
2 × 125g (5 oz) cartons natural yogurt
4 egg yolks
2½ teaspoons lemon juice
Seasoning

Number of servings: 4-6

Method
1. Whisk the yogurt, egg yolks and lemon juice together in a double saucepan (or basin standing over pan of gently simmering water).
2. Cook the sauce for about 15 minutes stirring frequently, until it thickens.
3. Season and serve with leeks or asparagus.

Quick Cream Sauce

For a quick sauce add 2 tablespoons of cream to any flavour of condensed soup. Season and heat.

Sweet White Sauce

Ingredients
25g (1oz) Scottish butter
25g (1oz) cornflour
280ml ($\frac{1}{2}$ pint) milk
25g (1oz) caster sugar
1 egg yolk

Number of servings: 4-6

Method
1. Blend cornflour with the milk in a saucepan. Add butter and heat, stirring continuously until sauce thickens and boils.
2. Stir in sugar and egg yolk. Serve hot or cold.

Variations
Brandy Sauce: Add 2 tablespoons brandy with sugar and egg yolk. Serve with Christmas pudding.
Orange or Lemon Sauce: Add finely grated rind of 1 orange or 1 lemon to milk. Serve with fruit pies or puddings.
Chocolate Sauce: Add 50g (2 oz) grated plain chocolate with sugar and egg yolk. Stir to melt chocolate. Serve with baked or steamed puddings.

Liqueur Sauces

Ingredients
140ml ($\frac{1}{4}$ pt) double cream
140ml ($\frac{1}{4}$ pt) single cream
1 egg white, stiffly beaten
Required liqueur

Number of servings: 6

Method
1. Add liqueur and stiffly beaten egg white to creams.
2. Whip creams together until thick.

This makes a softly stiff cream which is ideal for "dolloping" onto desserts, such as fresh fruit salad.

Suggested Liqueur Flavourings
1. 2 tablespoons Kirsch + 2 teaspoons juice from maraschino cherries.
2. 2 tablespoons Grand Marnier or Cointreau and a little grated orange rind.
3. 2 tablespoons Scotch Whisky + 2 tablespoons honey mixed with 1 tablespoon lemon juice.
4. 2 tablespoons Rum + a little grated orange or lemon rind.
5. 2 tablespoons Creme de Cacao or Tia Maria + 1 teaspoon strong black coffee.
6. 4 tablespoons Heather Cream Liqueur.

Arenberg Sauce

Ingredients
2 egg yolks
40g (1$\frac{1}{2}$ oz) sugar
70ml ($\frac{1}{8}$ pint) water
560ml (1 pint) double cream
$\frac{1}{4}$ teaspoon vanilla essence

Number of servings: 4-6

Method
1. Whisk the egg yolks, sugar, water and essence together in a bowl over warm water, until thick.
2. Whisk until cold, then add cream and continue whisking until it has a light consistency.

Serve as a coating sauce with fresh pears. (Peel, halve and core the pears then poach them gently in sugar and water). Tinned pear halves which have been drained, may also be used.

Butterscotch Sauce

Ingredients
50g (2 oz) Scottish butter
50g (2 oz) soft brown sugar
2 tablespoons golden syrup
1 × 200g (7 oz) tin condensed milk

Number of servings: 8

Method
1. Place butter, sugar and syrup in a double saucepan and heat gently until sugar has melted.
2. Add condensed milk and cook for a further 2-3 minutes, stirring all the time. Serve hot or cold with ice cream.

N.B. For a special occasion substitute 6 tablespoons Heather Cream Liqueur for the condensed milk.

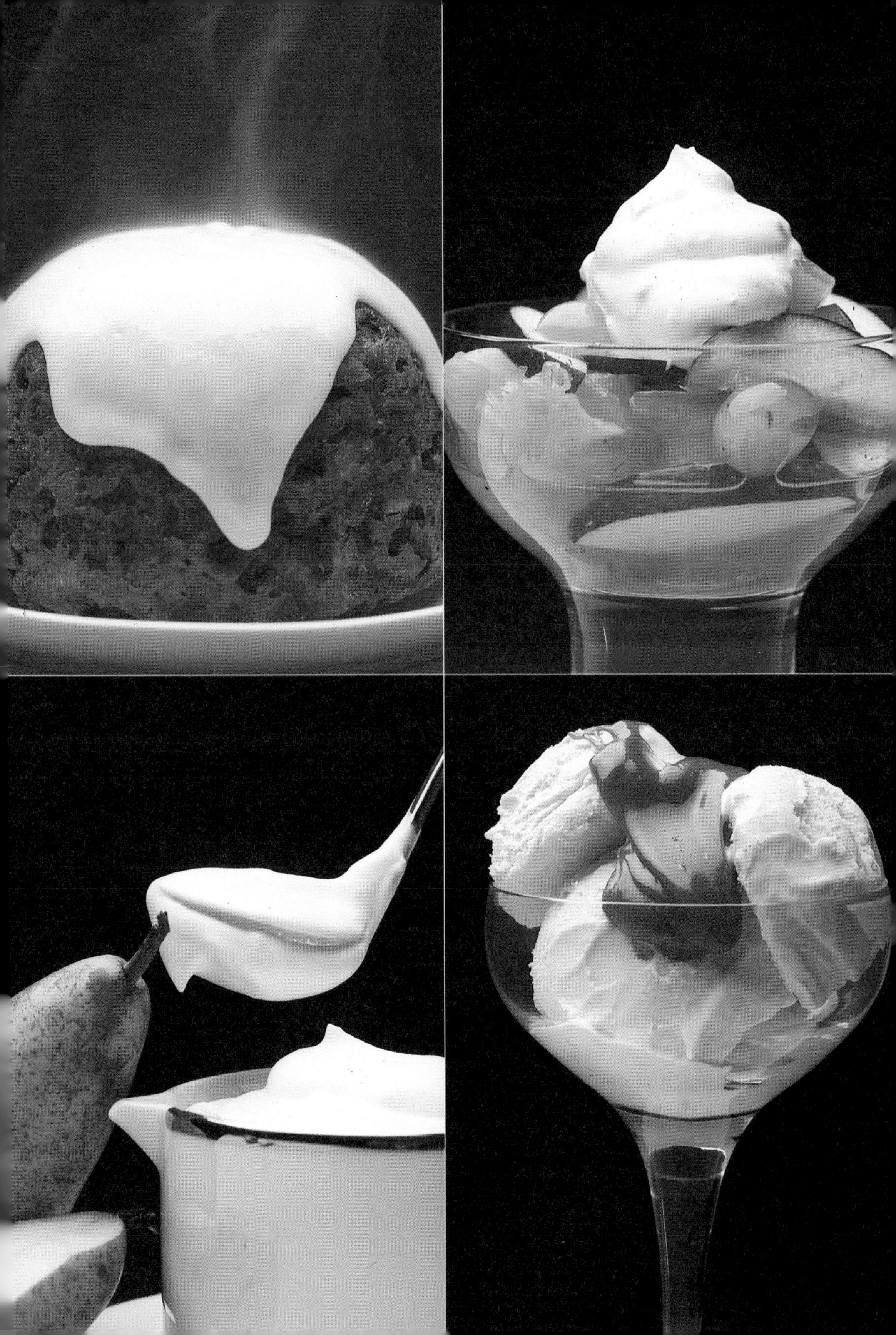

Casseroled Potatoes

Ingredients
450g (1 lb) potatoes
2 onions
25g (1 oz) Scottish butter
70 ml ($\frac{1}{8}$ pint) chicken stock
140 ml ($\frac{1}{4}$ pint) milk
Seasoning
Pinch grated nutmeg

Oven temperature: 190°C/375°F/No.5
Position in oven: centre
Time in oven: 1$\frac{1}{4}$ hours
Number of servings: 4

Method
1. Slice the onions and cook in butter until they are transparent.
2. Peel and slice the potatoes, place in an ovenproof dish together with the onions and sprinkle with salt, pepper and grated nutmeg.
3. Add the stock and milk and bake in oven.

Ratatouille

Ingredients
1 large aubergine, sliced
100g (4 oz) Scottish butter
1 large onion, sliced
1 clove garlic, finely chopped
225g (8 oz) courgettes, sliced
1 green pepper, cored, seeded & sliced
1 red pepper, cored, seeded & sliced
225g (8 oz) tomatoes, skinned & sliced
Seasoning
1 tablespoon chopped parsley
100g (4 oz) Scottish cheddar cheese, grated

Oven temperature: 180°C/350°F/No.4
Position in oven: Centre
Time in oven: 1 hour
Number of servings: 4

Method

1. Sprinkle aubergine slices with salt and leave to drain in a colander for half an hour. Wash, then dry well with kitchen towel.
2. Melt the butter in a large saucepan; add onion and garlic and fry for 2-3 minutes. Add courgettes, aubergine, green and red pepper and tomatoes. Season well with salt and black pepper then stir in the parsley. Simmer gently for a few minutes.
3. Place vegetable mixture in a large casserole, sprinkle with cheese and bake in oven. Serve hot with grilled or roast meat or fish.

Cheddar Tomatoes

Ingredients
4 good sized tomatoes
25g (1 oz) rolled oats
25g (1 oz) Scottish Cheddar cheese, grated
1 tablespoon chopped parsley
25g (1 oz) walnuts, chopped
Seasoning
Little cream

Oven temperature: 180°C/350°F/No.4
Position in oven: centre
Time in oven: 20-25 minutes
Number of servings: 4

Method

1. Cut tops off tomatoes and scoop out insides into a bowl, remove cores of tomatoes and discard.
2. Mix oats, cheese, parsley and nuts with pulp from tomatoes, then add seasoning and a little cream to give a moist consistency.
3. Fill tomatoes with filling, place tops back on and bake in oven.

Stuffed Peppers

Ingredients
4 green peppers
100g (4 oz) long grain rice, cooked
150g (6 oz) Scottish cheddar cheese, grated
50g (2 oz) mushrooms, cooked and sliced
½ teaspoon mustard
1 × 125g (5 oz) carton soured cream
Seasoning
25g (1 oz) Scottish butter

Oven temperature: 180°C/350°F/No.4
Position in oven: Centre
Time in oven: 15 minutes
Number of servings: 4

Method

1. Cut tops off the peppers and remove seeds. Put peppers in a pan, cover with boiling salted water and simmer for 2 minutes. Remove from pan and drain upside down on kitchen paper.
2. Place rice in a bowl then mix in two thirds of grated cheese, and all mushrooms, mustard and cream. Season.

3. Stand peppers in a shallow ovenproof dish. Fill with equal amounts of rice mixture.
4. Put a knob of butter on top of each and sprinkle with the remaining cheese. Cover dish with foil and bake in oven.

Baked Potatoes

1. Choose large potatoes of an even size.
2. Scrub them and prick them then place on grid of oven shelves.
3. Bake in oven until potatoes feel tender when gently pressed.
4. Remove from oven and cut a large cross on top of each potato.
5. Hold potato in a clean teatowel and squeeze firmly to enlarge cut.
6. Serve hot with lots of Scottish butter.

Oven temperature: 220°C/425°F/No.7
Position in oven: above centre
Time in oven: 1-1¼ hours

Suggested Fillings:

(a) Cottage cheese and pineapple
(b) Soured cream and chopped chives
(c) Grated Scottish Cheddar cheese and chopped tomato, onion or ham
(d) Various flavoured butters (see Corn on the Cob recipe. P25)

Method

1. Bake the potatoes, then scoop out the cooked potato, leaving skin intact.
2. Mash potatoes in a bowl and combine with filling. Season.
3. Divide filling equally and fill potato shells.
4. If liked, serve wrapped individually in tin foil.

Stuffed Courgettes

Ingredients

3 medium sized courgettes
50g (2 oz) Scottish butter
25g (1 oz) flour
280 ml (½ pint) milk
4-6 syboes or 1 small onion, chopped
1 teaspoon tomato purée or ketchup
150g (6 oz) prawns
1 tablespoon dry white wine
100g (4 oz) Scottish Cheddar cheese, grated

Oven temperature: 220°C/425°F/No.7
Position in oven: centre
Time in oven: 10-14 minutes
Number of servings: 4

Method

1. Trim ends of courgettes, cook whole in boiling salted water for 5 minutes. Drain then cover with cold water.
2. Make a white sauce with half the butter and all the flour and milk (see Step by Step Cookery Page 114). Add half the cheese and stir until it melts.

3. Half courgettes lengthwise. Scoop out and roughly chop flesh.
4. Melt the remaining butter add the syboes and cook for a few minutes. Add the courgette flesh and tomato purée. Season then cook for 2-3 minutes. Stir in prawns and wine.
5. Place the courgette skins in a shallow ovenproof serving dish. Fill them with the prawn mixture.
6. Pour the cheese sauce over the courgettes, sprinkle with rest of cheese and brown in oven.

Cauliflower Crunch

Ingredients

1 large cauliflower, cut into sprigs
2 eggs (hard boiled)
1 onion, sliced
50g (2 oz) Scottish butter
100g (4 oz) mushrooms, sliced
25g (1 oz) flour
140ml ($\frac{1}{4}$ pint) milk
1 × 125g (5 oz) carton natural yogurt
Seasoning
100g (4 oz) Scottish cheddar cheese, grated
25g (1 oz) fresh white breadcrumbs

Oven temperature: 180°C/350°F/No.4
Position in oven: Centre
Time in oven: 10-15 minutes
Number of servings: 4

Method

1. Cook cauliflower sprigs in boiling salted water for 5-10 minutes.
2. Melt half the butter, add onion and mushrooms and cook for 2-3 minutes until soft.

3. Make a white sauce with remaining butter, flour and milk, (see Step by Step Cookery p.114). Blend in yogurt, seasoning and half the grated cheese.
4. Place cauliflower in the base of a casserole dish; chop eggs and sprinkle over cauliflower. Place onion and mushroom mixture on top then coat with sauce.
5. Mix remaining cheese and breadcrumbs together. Sprinkle over cauliflower, dot with butter and brown in oven.

Vegetable Pilaff

Ingredients

100g (4 oz) carrots, thinly sliced
100g (4 oz) cauliflower, cut into sprigs
50g (2 oz) leeks, sliced
25g (1 oz) Scottish butter
75g (3 oz) long grain rice
280ml ($\frac{1}{2}$ pint) chicken stock
$\frac{1}{2}$ teaspoon paprika
$\frac{1}{2}$ teaspoon ground cinnamon
$\frac{1}{2}$ teaspoon ground cloves
$\frac{1}{2}$ green pepper, chopped
1 tablespoon chopped parsley

Oven temperature: 150°C/300°F/No.2
Position in oven: Centre
Time in oven: 15-20 minutes
Number of servings: 4

Method

1. Melt butter, fry carrots, cauliflower and leeks gently for 2-3 minutes in a large casserole.
2. Add rice and fry for a further 3 minutes, stirring all the time.

3. Blend in stock and bring to the boil. Season and add spices.
4. Cover with greased greaseproof paper and cook in oven until all stock has been absorbed.
5. Stir in pepper and parsley and serve.

Salads

Waldorf Salad

Ingredients
3 red eating apples
2 tablespoons lemon juice
2 tablespoons single cream
1 × 125 g (5 oz) carton natural yogurt
¼ cucumber, washed and diced
75g (3 oz) Scottish cheddar cheese, diced
25g (1 oz) walnuts, chopped
Seasoning
1 lettuce

Number of servings: 4

Method
1. Wash and core apples, slice one finely and dice remainder, then dip in lemon juice.
2. Mix cheese, cucumber, walnuts and diced apple into yogurt and cream. Season.
3. Line a bowl with lettuce leaves, pile salad in centre and garnish with apple slices and a sprig of parsley.

Coleslaw

Ingredients
1 tablespoon mayonnaise
1 tablespoon milk
2 tablespoons natural yogurt
50g (2 oz) Scottish cheddar cheese, grated
1 carrot, grated
225g (8 oz) white cabbage, shredded
Seasoning
Sliced cucumber and cress to garnish

Number of servings: 4

Method
1. Place mayonnaise, milk, yogurt and seasoning in a bowl and mix well.
2. Add grated cheese, carrot and cabbage and toss in dressing.
3. Serve in a bowl garnished with cucumber and cress.

Winter Salad

Ingredients
2 red apples, chopped
100g (4 oz) Scottish cheddar cheese, cubed
100g (4 oz) cooked ham, cubed
1 small tin sliced peaches, drained and cubed
50g (2 oz) salted peanuts
50g (2 oz) sultanas
1 × 125g (5 oz) carton natural yogurt
1 lettuce or winter cabbage, washed
Tomato slices to garnish

Number of servings: 4

Method
1. Mix apples, cheese, ham, peaches, nuts and sultanas in yogurt.
2. Line a serving dish with lettuce or cabbage leaves, pile salad in centre and garnish with slices of tomato.

Marshmallow Salad

Ingredients
1 × 125g (5 oz) carton natural yogurt
Seasoning
2 oranges, peeled and chopped
1 × 225g (8 oz) tin pineapple chunks, drained
100g (4 oz) marshmallows, chopped
50g (2 oz) dessicated coconut to garnish

Number of servings: 4

Method
1. Season yogurt. Mix oranges, pineapple and marshmallows in yogurt.
2. Serve sprinkled with coconut.

N.B. This is also delicious served as a dessert.

Summer Salad

Ingredients
225g (8 oz) fresh strawberries
½ cucumber
1 × 125g (5 oz) carton cottage cheese
25g (1 oz) walnuts, chopped
Salt and black pepper
1 × 125g (5 oz) carton soured cream
1 lettuce

Number
of servings: 4

Method
1. Wash and hull strawberries, and cut into quarters, reserving a few halved strawberries for decoration.
2. Wash and dice cucumber, but reserve a few slices for decoration.
3. Mix cottage cheese, chopped walnuts, cucumber and strawberries into the soured cream. Mix well and season.
4. Serve on a bed of lettuce, garnished with cucumber slices and strawberry halves.

Chicken & Almond Salad

Ingredients
100g (4 oz) raisins
75g (3 oz) Scottish cheddar cheese, cubed
1 tablespoon grated onion
100g (4 oz) cooked chicken, chopped
3 sticks celery, chopped
Seasoning
2 tablespoons mayonnaise
140ml (¼ pt) double cream, lightly whipped
1 tablespoon chopped parsley
50g (2 oz) browned almonds } garnish
1 lettuce

Number of
servings: 4

Method
1. Blend mayonnaise into whipped cream. Season.
2. Combine all ingredients together and add to mayonnaise and cream, mix well.
3. Serve on a bed of lettuce and garnish with parsley and almonds.

Indian Salad

Ingredients
50g (2 oz) long grain rice
125ml (4 fl oz) double cream
125g (5 oz) cottage cheese
2 dessertspoons curry powder
2 dessertspoons mayonnaise
Seasoning
3 pineapple rings, cubed
50g (2 oz) sultanas
2 hard boiled eggs, chopped
1 hard boiled egg, sliced, to garnish
Lettuce and parsley to garnish

Number of
servings: 4

Method
1. Cook rice in boiling salted water for 12 minutes.
2. Whip cream lightly, stir in cottage cheese, curry powder and mayonnaise. Season.
3. Add cooked rice, pineapple, sultanas and chopped hard boiled egg.
4. Arrange on a bed of lettuce and garnish with egg and parsley.

Celery & Nut Salad

Ingredients
2 tablespoons clear honey
Pinch of grated nutmeg
Seasoning
1 × 125g (5 oz) carton soured cream
1 tablespoon lemon juice
1 lettuce
4 carrots, grated
1 red pepper, thinly sliced
1 dessert apple, cored and diced
50g (2 oz) walnuts, chopped
50g (2 oz) almonds, chopped
4 sticks of celery, diced

Number of servings: 4

Method

1. For the dressing, mix together the honey, nutmeg and seasoning.
2. Whisk in the soured cream, then stir in the lemon juice.
3. Line a bowl with lettuce leaves.
4. Mix carrots, red pepper, apple, celery and nuts with the dressing and pile on the lettuce leaves.

Potato Salad

Ingredients
450g (1 lb) small new potatoes, cooked
140ml ($\frac{1}{4}$ pint) mayonnaise
$\frac{1}{2}$ × 125g (5 oz) carton soured cream
1 teaspoon parsley, chopped
1 teaspoon chives, chopped
Seasoning
Chopped parsley to garnish

Number of servings: 4

Method
1. Cut the potatoes into cubes.
2. Mix the mayonnaise with the soured cream, parsley and chives. Season.
3. Add the potatoes and stir gently to coat them.
4. To serve, garnish with parsley.

N.B. Soured cream can be made by adding 1 teaspoon of lemon juice to a 140ml (5 fl.oz) carton of single cream.

Green Salad

Ingredients
1 lettuce, washed
1 large onion, finely sliced
$\frac{1}{2}$ green pepper, deseeded and cut into strips
$\frac{1}{2}$ cucumber, sliced
6-8 tablespoons olive oil
Seasoning and dry mustard
2 tablespoons wine vinegar
4 tablespoons Scottish cheddar cheese, grated

Number of servings: 4

Method
1. Place lettuce leaves in base of serving dish. Arrange sliced cucumber and onion and strips of green pepper on top.
2. To make dressing put oil, seasoning and mustard into a bowl and beat until smooth. Gradually beat in vinegar. Continue beating until the dressing thickens.
3. Pour dressing over salad and sprinkle with grated cheese.

Main Courses

Baked Yogurt Chicken

Ingredients

4 chicken portions
1 tablespoon plain flour
1 teaspoon curry powder
1 teaspoon salt
1 teaspoon ground ginger
½ crushed clove of garlic (optional)
2 teaspoons paprika
50g (2 oz) Scottish butter
140ml (¼ pint) chicken stock
1 × 125g (5 oz) carton natural yogurt

Oven temperature: 170°C/325°F/No.3
Position in oven: Centre
Time in oven: 1 hour 15 minutes
Number of servings: 4

Method

1. Make up seasoned flour by mixing all dry ingredients together.
2. Coat chicken portions in seasoned flour and fry in butter until golden on all sides. Remove and place in a casserole dish sprinkling over any excess flour.
3. Pour over chicken stock and cook for 1¼ hours in a warm oven 170°C/325°F/No.3
4. Remove chicken from casserole and keep warm. Blend yogurt into juices. Heat through but do not boil. Serve chicken coated with yogurt sauce.

Creamy Mushroom Steak

Ingredients

450g (1lb) stewing steak, cubed
40g (1½ oz) Scottish butter
75g (3 oz) mushrooms, sliced
1 × 298g (10½ oz) tin condensed mushroom soup
140 ml (¼ pt) milk
Seasoning

Oven temperature: 150°C/300°F/No.2
Position in oven: Centre
Time in oven: 2½ hours
Number of servings: 4

Method

1. Brown stewing steaks in butter, add mushrooms and cook for 1-2 minutes.
2. Combine soup and milk and add to steak. Season.
3. Place in a 1 litre (2 pt) ovenproof dish and bake slowly until tender.

Curried Ham Risotto

Ingredients

100g (4 oz) Scottish butter
1 medium onion, chopped
150g (6 oz) long grain rice
560ml (1 pt) ham stock
2 tomatoes, skinned and chopped
2 teaspoons curry powder
Seasoning
100g (4 oz) mushrooms, sliced and fried in butter
150g (6 oz) ham, cooked and diced
1 × 225g (8 oz) tin pineapple chunks, drained

Number of servings: 4

Method

1. Melt butter in pan and fry onion lightly then add rice and cook for a few minutes.
2. Add stock, tomatoes, curry powder and seasoning and bring to the boil.
3. Cover and simmer gently for 20-25 minutes or until all stock is absorbed.
4. Add cooked mushrooms, ham and pineapple chunks and heat thoroughly. Serve at once in a hot serving dish.

Chicken Smetana

Ingredients
4 chicken joints
50g (2 oz) Scottish butter
2 syboes, chopped
1 wine glass dry white wine
Seasoning

Sauce: **3 syboes, finely chopped**
1 large wine glass dry white wine
1 dessertspoonful flour
1 × 125g (5 oz) carton soured cream

Number of servings: 4

Method
1. Heat the butter in a large pan and slowly brown the joints. Add chopped syboes, wine and seasoning.
2. Cover and simmer gently for 45-50 minutes, turning the joints from time to time.
3. When the joints are cooked, remove and arrange on a serving dish. Keep warm.

Strain liquid and reserve for sauce.
4. To make the sauce: cook the 3 finely chopped syboes in the wine until the wine is reduced by half. Strain liquid and discard the syboes.
5. Carefully blend flour with liquid from chicken then add the reduced wine and cream. Bring slowly to the boil, stirring all the time until the sauce is thick and creamy. Taste for seasoning. Spoon sauce over joints and serve.

Mince & Vegetable Hotpot

Ingredients
450g (1 lb) cooked potato, sliced
340g (12 oz) minced beef
50g (2 oz) flour, seasoned
1 onion, chopped
15g ($\frac{1}{2}$ oz) Scottish butter
290g (10 oz) tin condensed vegetable soup
4 tablespoons stock
1 egg
1 × 125g (5 oz) carton natural yogurt
Seasoning
Paprika pepper, if liked

Oven temperature: 190°C/375°F/No.5
Position in oven: Centre
Time in oven: 15-20 minutes
Number of servings: 4

Method
1. Line a deep casserole dish with the sliced cooked potatoes.

2. Mix minced beef with half the seasoned flour. Fry the mince and onion in butter for 10-15 minutes. Add soup and stock and simmer for 15 minutes.
3. Pour mince mixture over potatoes.
4. Beat egg together with the yogurt and remaining flour. Season and pour over mince.
5. Bake uncovered in a fairly hot oven for 15-20 minutes. Serve sprinkled with paprika pepper.

Pork & Pineapple Curry

Ingredients

1 large onion, chopped
40g ($1\frac{1}{2}$ oz) Scottish butter
450g (1 lb) pork fillet, cubed
25g (1 oz) flour
1-2 tablespoons curry powder
1 × 225g (8 oz) tin pineapple chunks
1 tablespoon tomato purée
50g (2 oz) sultanas
280ml ($\frac{1}{2}$ pint) juice from pineapple and water
140ml ($\frac{1}{4}$ pint) milk
Seasoning
150g (6 oz) long grain rice

Number of servings: 4

Method

1. Fry onions in butter until soft, then add pork and fry on all sides until lightly browned.
2. Stir in flour and curry powder, add pineapple pieces, tomato purée, sultanas, pineapple juice, water and milk. Bring to the boil and simmer, stirring occasionally, for 20-25 minutes, or until meat is tender.
3. Season and serve on a bed of freshly boiled rice.

Suggested accompaniments to serve with curry:

Mango chutney, sliced cucumber, sliced banana, onion rings, tomato slices and dessicated coconut.

Lamb Goulash

Ingredients
50g (2 oz) Scottish butter
2 onions, chopped
1 garlic clove, chopped
50g (2 oz) bacon, chopped
450g (1 lb) stewing lamb, cubed
1 green pepper, chopped
1 tablespoon paprika
1 tablespoon tomato purée
1 × 198g (7 oz) tin tomatoes
Seasoning
1 × 125g (5 oz) carton soured cream

Number of servings: 4

Method
1. Melt butter and gently fry onion, garlic and bacon.
2. Add lamb and brown well.
3. Add chopped pepper, paprika, tomato purée and tinned tomatoes. Season.
4. Cover, bring to boil, then simmer for about 1 hour (or until meat is tender).
5. Stir in soured cream and heat through.
6. Sprinkle with parsley and serve with pitta bread

Pork Cream Amontillado

Ingredients
450g (1 lb) pork fillet, cubed
75g (3 oz) Scottish butter
100g (4 oz) mushrooms, sliced
1 onion, sliced
1 green pepper, sliced
2 tablespoons flour
1 tablespoon tomato purée
280 ml ($\frac{1}{2}$ pint) chicken stock
$\frac{1}{4}$ teaspoon mixed herbs
Seasoning
4 tablespoons sherry
2 tablespoons double cream
1 teaspoon chopped parsley
150g (6 oz) rice or noodles

Number of servings: 4

Method

1. Melt butter, add pork and lightly brown. Remove from pan.

2. Add mushrooms, onion and pepper to pan and cook for 2-3 minutes.
3. Stir in flour, tomato purée, stock, mixed herbs and seasoning.
4. Bring to the boil, return pork to the pan and simmer gently for 20 minutes.
5. Just before serving, stir in sherry and double cream.
6. Sprinkle with parsley and serve with rice or noodles.

Beef Stroganoff

Ingredients
550g (1$\frac{1}{4}$ lb) rump or fillet steak
Seasoning
1 small onion, chopped
75g (3 oz) Scottish butter
225g (8 oz) button mushrooms
3 tablespoons white wine
140ml ($\frac{1}{4}$ pint) double cream
150g (6 oz) rice or noodles to serve
Chopped parsley

Number of servings: 4

Method

1. Beat steak with rolling pin and cut into strips 1 cm ($\frac{1}{2}$ inch) wide.
2. Gently fry onion in half the butter for 5 minutes.
3. Add strips of steak and fry for a further 10 minutes, turning all the time. Remove steak to plate.
4. Place remaining butter in pan, add mushrooms and cook for 3 minutes. Return

steak to pan, season, stir in wine and cook for a further five minutes. Reduce heat and add cream before serving. Do not boil. Taste for seasoning.

5. Serve with rice or noodles and garnish with chopped parsley.

Herbie Liver

Ingredients

340g (12 oz) ox or lamb's liver
280ml ($\frac{1}{2}$ pint) milk
25g (1 oz) flour
Seasoning
40g ($1\frac{1}{2}$ oz) Scottish butter
1 onion, thinly sliced
140ml ($\frac{1}{4}$ pint) stock
2 tablespoons tomato purée
1 clove garlic, finely chopped (optional)
$\frac{1}{4}$ teaspoon mixed herbs
2 tablespoons double cream
Chopped parsley to decorate

Number of servings: 4

Method

1. Cut liver into small pieces and coat in seasoned flour.
2. Melt butter in a frying pan. Add the liver and brown lightly. Add onion and cook for one minute.
3. Gradually stir in the stock, milk, tomato purée, garlic (if liked) and herbs. Bring sauce to the boil, stirring all the time. Cover and simmer for 15-30 minutes until the liver is tender.
4. Season to taste. Garnish by trickling a little cream over the liver and sprinkle with chopped parsley.

N.B. This dish can be served with boiled rice

Veal Escalopes au Gratin

Ingredients

4 escalopes veal
50g (2 oz) Scottish butter
2 teaspoons olive oil
Sauce: 225g (8 oz) cottage cheese
50g (2 oz) Scottish cheddar cheese, finely grated
3 sticks celery, chopped
100g (4 oz) lean ham, chopped
1 × 225g (8 oz) tin pineapple cubes, drained
Seasoning

Number of servings: 4

Method

1. Beat each piece of veal until very thin. Nick edges with scissors to prevent meat from curling up as it cooks.
2. Fry gently in hot butter and oil allowing about 5 minutes per side. Place in serving dish and keep warm in oven.
3. To make sauce, mix cottage cheese and cheddar cheese together. Add chopped celery, ham and pineapple cubes. Season to taste.
4. Spoon sauce over veal escalopes and grill for 2-3 minutes.

Note: This sauce is also ideal to serve with pork or turkey escalopes or chicken portions.

Cheeseburger Casserole

Ingredients

225g (8 oz) minced beef
100g (4 oz) Scottish cheddar cheese, grated
100g (4 oz) fresh white breadcrumbs
1 onion, chopped
Seasoning
1 egg, beaten
25g (1 oz) Scottish butter
25g (1 oz) flour, seasoned
290g ($10\frac{1}{2}$ oz) tin condensed tomato soup
2 tablespoons milk
75g (3 oz) Scottish cheddar cheese, grated } **topping**
450g (1 lb) potatoes, mashed } **topping**

Oven temperature: 200°C/400°F/No.6
Position in oven: Centre
Time in oven: 20-30 minutes
Number of servings: 4

Method

1. Mix minced beef, cheese, breadcrumbs, onion, egg and seasoning together and form into small balls and toss in seasoned flour.
2. Brown in melted butter and place in an ovenproof dish. Blend milk with soup and pour over meatballs.
3. Mix grated cheese through mashed potato. Taste for seasoning. Moisten the potato with a little milk, if required.
4. Pipe or spread potato over the meatballs and bake in fairly hot oven for 20 to 30 minutes..

Tripe & Onion Stew

Ingredients
450g (1 lb) cooked tripe
1 onion, roughly chopped
420ml ($\frac{3}{4}$ pint) milk
20g ($\frac{3}{4}$ oz) cornflour
25g (1 oz) Scottish butter
Chopped parsley

Number of servings: 4

Method

1. Cover tripe with milk, add onions and simmer until tender.
2. Blend cornflour with a little milk, add to tripe with butter. Bring to boil, stirring all the time; season and simmer for a few minutes.
3. Sprinkle with chopped parsley and serve with boiled potatoes.

Steaks Crème Napoleon

Ingredients
4 × 150g (6 oz) sirloin steaks
1 onion, finely chopped
50g (2 oz) Scottish butter
140ml ($\frac{1}{4}$ pt) red wine
100g (4 oz) mushrooms
1 tablespoon brandy
280ml ($\frac{1}{2}$ pt) double cream
150g (6 oz) long grain rice
Seasoning

Number of servings: 4

Method

1. Soak steak in red wine with half the chopped onion, overnight.
2. Fry the rest of the onion in butter, add steaks and cook over a high heat for 1 minute on each side.
3. Add red wine and mushrooms and cook steaks for 2-4 mins.
4. Add brandy to steaks and flame (i.e. pour the brandy over the steaks and ignite it. This gives flavour to the dish and at the same time reduces the alcohol content of the spirit. The brandy should be warmed before it is ignited).
5. Take out steaks, put in serving dish.
6. Add cream and heat through. Season.
7. Serve garnished with cooked rice.

Lunch and Supper Dishes

Underwood Pie

Ingredients

Pastry:	**150g (6 oz) flour** **50g (2 oz) Scottish butter** **50g (2 oz) Scottish cheddar cheese, grated** **Seasoning** **Little water to mix.**
Filling:	**50g (2 oz) breadcrumbs** **15g ($\frac{1}{2}$ oz) butter** **280ml ($\frac{1}{2}$ pt) milk** **1 egg, beaten** **50g (2 oz) Scottish cheddar cheese, grated** **1 teaspoon mixed herbs** **$\frac{1}{2}$ onion, grated** **Seasoning**

Oven temperature: 190°C/375°F/No. 5
Position in oven: Centre
Time in oven: 50 minutes
Number of servings: 6

Method

1. To make pastry, sieve flour and seasoning together. Rub in butter until mixture resembles fine breadcrumbs. Mix in cheese, Bind mixture together with sufficient water to make a stiff dough.
2. Roll out pastry and line six individual deep pastry cases or an 18cm (7 inch) flan case. Bake blind in oven at 190°C/375°F/No.5 for about 20 minutes.

To make filling

3. Heat milk and butter and pour over breadcrumbs. Mix in egg thoroughly and then add all other ingredients.
4. Divide mixture between pastry cases and bake in oven at 180°C/350°F/No. 4 for 30 minutes until set.

Herbie Pie

Ingredients
340g (12 oz) sausage meat
Mixed herbs to taste
50g (2 oz) streaky bacon, chopped
50g (2 oz) onion, chopped
Seasoning
150g (6 oz) Scottish cheddar cheese, grated
450g (1 lb) potatoes, mashed

Oven temperature: 180°C/350°F/No.4
Position in oven: Centre
Time in oven: 1 hour
Number of servings: 4

Method

1. Place sausage meat in base of ovenproof dish then sprinkle with mixed herbs.
2. Fry bacon and onion until soft and place over sausage meat, season.
3. Mix grated cheese with potato. Pipe or spread this over the top and bake in a moderate oven for 1 hour.

Cheddar Kebabs

Ingredients
100g (4 oz) chipolata sausages
8 button mushrooms
8 large pickled onions
$\frac{1}{4}$ cucumber, diced
4 tomatoes, quartered
150g (6 oz) Scottish cheddar cheese, cubed

Number of servings: 4

Method

1. Cut sausages in half and grill until cooked.
2. Blanch mushrooms in boiling water for 1 minute then plunge immediately into cold water.
3. Arrange sausages, onions, cucumber, mushrooms, tomatoes and cheese attractively on skewers.

Quickie Pizza

Ingredients

150g (6 oz) self raising flour
$\frac{1}{2}$ teaspoon salt
$\frac{1}{2}$ teaspoon mixed herbs
40g (1$\frac{1}{2}$ oz) Scottish butter
6 tablespoons milk
1 small onion, finely chopped
150g (6 oz) tomatoes, skinned and sliced
25g (1 oz) Scottish butter
Teaspoon parsley, chopped
Seasoning
100g (4 oz) Scottish cheddar cheese, grated or sliced
2 rashers streaky bacon, cut into narrow strips

Oven temperature:	220°C/425°F/No.7
Position in oven:	Centre
Time in oven:	25-30 minutes
Number of servings:	4

Method

1. Sift flour and salt in a bowl. Add herbs. Rub in butter until mixture resembles fine breadcrumbs. Mix to a soft dough with milk.

2. Knead dough lightly and roll out, on a floured board, to 1 large or 4 individual rounds $\frac{1}{2}$cm ($\frac{1}{4}$ in) thick. Place on a greased baking tray.
3. For topping, fry onion and tomatoes in butter until soft. Add parsley and season well.
4. Place mixture over pizza base and top with cheese. Decorate with strips of bacon in a lattice pattern. Bake in a hot oven for 25-30 minutes.

Cheese Bakewell Tart

Ingredients

100g (4 oz) flour
Seasoning and dried mustard
25g (1 oz) Scottish butter
25g (1 oz) Scottish cheddar cheese, grated
Water to mix
2 tomatoes, sliced
Sauce: **25g (1 oz) Scottish butter**
25g (1 oz) flour
280ml ($\frac{1}{2}$ pint) milk
2 eggs, separated
100g (4 oz) Scottish cheddar cheese, grated
50g (2 oz) fresh breadcrumbs
Seasoning

Oven temperature:	190°C/375°F/No.5
Position in oven:	Centre
Time in oven:	45 minutes
Number of servings:	4

Method

1. For pastry, sieve flour and seasonings together. Rub in butter until mixture resembles fine breadcrumbs. Mix in cheese, then bind together with sufficient water to make a stiff dough.
2. Line an 18cm (7 in) flan ring with pastry and cover bottom with tomato slices.
3. Make up a basic white sauce (see Step by Step Cookery page 114) then beat in egg yo Add cheese, breadcrumbs and seasoning.
4. Whisk egg whites until soft peaks form and fold into cheese mixture. Pour into flan case and bake in a fairly hot oven for 45 minutes until golden brown.

Prawn Roulade

Ingredients

25g (1 oz) Scottish butter
25g (1 oz) flour
140ml ($\frac{1}{4}$ pt) milk
75g (3 oz) Scottish cheddar cheese, grated
3 eggs, separated
Seasoning
Filling: 50g (2 oz) Scottish cheddar cheese, grated & mixed with 50g (2 oz) prawns

Topping: 25g (1 oz) Scottish cheddar cheese, grated

Prawns and parsley to garnish

Oven temperature:	180°C/350°F/No.4
Position in oven:	Centre
Time in oven:	15 minutes
Number of servings:	4

Method

1. Grease a swiss roll tin and line with greased wax paper.
2. Melt butter in pan, add flour and cook until smooth.
3. Gradually add milk and bring to the boil, stirring. Reduce heat and simmer. Stir until mixture thickens and leaves bottom of pan. Season.
4. Beat in grated cheese. Whisk in egg yolks and beat mixture well.
5. Whisk egg whites until stiff and fold carefully into mixture.
6. Pour into greased and lined swiss roll tin and bake in oven.
7. Turn out onto greased wax paper, resting on a damp towel. Remove paper from base, spread quickly with prepared filling. Roll into fairly tight roll.
8. Leave soufflé in towel for few minutes, then remove wax paper. Top with grated cheese and grill.

Serve garnished with prawns and parsley.

Neapolitan Macaroni

Ingredients

225g (8 oz) macaroni
50g (2 oz) lean bacon, chopped
1 small onion, chopped
40g ($1\frac{1}{2}$ oz) Scottish butter
225g (8 oz) tomatoes, skinned and sliced
140ml ($\frac{1}{4}$ pint) stock
50g (2 oz) Scottish cheddar cheese, grated
Seasoning

Number of servings: 4

Method

1. Cook macaroni in boiling salted water for 12 minutes. Drain well.
2. Fry bacon and onion in butter until cooked, then add sliced, skinned tomato. Add stock and cooked macaroni and mix well. Season.
3. Turn into a preheated ovenproof dish, sprinkle with grated cheese and brown under grill.

Cheesy French Toast

Ingredients

2 slices bread
25g (1 oz) Scottish butter
1 egg
4 tablespoons milk
Seasoning
100g (4 oz) Scottish cheddar cheese, sliced or grated.

Number of servings: 1

Method

1. Heat butter in frying pan.
2. Beat egg with milk, season.
3. Dip one slice of bread in beaten egg and cover with cheese.
4. Dip other slice of bread in egg and place on top of cheese.
5. Fry in hot butter until golden brown.

Ingredients

4 hard boiled eggs
225g (8 oz) Scottish cheddar cheese, grated
40g ($1\frac{1}{2}$ oz) flour
Seasoning
1 egg, beaten
2 tablespoons milk
Dried breadcrumbs, to coat

Number of servings: 4

Method

1. Mix grated cheese, flour and seasoning. Add beaten egg and milk and beat well.
2. Using wet hands, coat hard boiled eggs in cheese mix.
3. Coat eggs with breadcrumbs and fry in deep fat for 5-7 minutes.

Serve hot or cold with salad.

Corn & Tuna Bake

Ingredients

100g (4 oz) sweetcorn
1 × 75g (3 oz) tin tuna fish, drained
1 onion, finely chopped
1 tablespoon plain flour
280ml ($\frac{1}{2}$ pint) milk
2 eggs, beaten
Seasoning
25g (1 oz) cornflakes
75g (3 oz) Scottish cheddar cheese, grated

Oven temperature: 190°C/375°F/No.5
Position in oven: Centre
Time in oven: 40 minutes
Number of servings: 4

Method

1. Mix the sweetcorn, flaked tuna fish and chopped onion together.
2. Blend the flour with the milk and add beaten egg and seasoning.
3. Add the corn mixture to the beaten eggs and milk and pour into an ovenproof dish.
4. Mix the cornflakes and cheese together and sprinkle over the mixture.
5. Bake in a fairly hot oven for about 40 minutes.

Cheese Rice Loaf

Ingredients

225g (8 oz) long grain rice
1 small onion, chopped
50g (2 oz) Scottish butter
1 teaspoon curry powder
75g (3 oz) Scottish cheddar cheese, grated
1 small tin tomatoes
50g (2 oz) mixed vegetables
2 eggs, beaten
Seasoning
1 tomato, sliced to garnish
Sprigs of parsley to garnish

Oven temperature: 180°C/350°F/No.4
Position in oven: Centre
Time in oven: 1½-2 hours
Number of servings: 4-6

Method

1. Cook rice in boiling salted water for 12 minutes. Drain well.
2. Fry onion in butter and add curry powder. Mix in cheese, tomatoes, mixed vegetables and rice and bind together with eggs.
3. Pour into a 1kg (2 lb) buttered loaf tin and cook in a moderate oven for 1½-2 hours. Serve hot or cold garnished with sprigs of parsley and tomato slices cut into quarters.

Fritter Cakes

Ingredients

225g (8 oz) minced beef
1 onion, chopped
50g (2 oz) flour
Seasoning to taste
1 egg, beaten
140ml (¼ pint) milk
Scottish butter, for frying

Number of servings: 4

Method

1. Mix the mince and onion together.
2. Sieve the flour, salt and pepper and gradually blend in the beaten egg and milk to make a smooth batter.
3. Stir the mince and onion mixture into the batter and leave aside for ½ hour.
4. Heat butter (½cm (¼ in) deep) in a frying pan. Drop rounded tablespoons of the mixture into the hot butter.
5. Reduce heat and fry fritter cakes for about 15 minutes, turning from time to time, until the batter is crisp and the meat is cooked through. Serve hot in white or wheaten rolls.

Quiche Lorraine

Ingredients
Cheese Pastry:

100g (4 oz) plain flour
Salt, pepper and mustard
50g (2 oz) Scottish butter
40g (1½ oz) Scottish Cheddar cheese grated
1 tablespoon cold water to mix

Filling:

50g (2 oz) bacon chopped } cook together in
1 onion or 8 syboes sliced } 15g (½ oz) butter
50g (2 oz) Scottish Cheddar cheese grated
1 egg
1 egg yolk
Salt, pepper, pinch of nutmeg
140ml (¼ pint) single cream

Oven temperature: 190°C/375°F/No. 5
Position in oven: Centre
Time in oven: 45-50 minutes
Number of servings: 4

Method

1. Make up pastry by sieving flour and seasonings together, then rub in butter. Mix in cheese then bind together with as little water as possible.
2. Roll out pastry and line an 18cm (7 inch) flan ring. Bake "blind" in a fairly hot oven 190°C/375°F/No.5 for about 20 minutes.
3. Beat the egg and extra yolk in a bowl, add the cheese, seasoning and cream. Mix in cooked bacon and onion.
4. Pour into the flan case and bake at 170°C/325°F/No. 3 for about 30 minutes. Serve hot or cold.

N.B. To bake blind, prick the base of the pastry with a fork. Line with a round of greaseproof paper sufficient to cover sides and base. Fill ring with dried peas (this prevents pastry rising). Cook for 15 minutes. Take out of oven, remove peas and paper. Return to oven for a further 5 minutes.

Cheese & Parsley Soufflé

Ingredients
25g (1 oz) Scottish butter
25g (1 oz) flour
140ml ($\frac{1}{4}$ pt) milk
75g (3 oz) Scottish cheddar cheese, grated
1 tablespoon parsley, chopped
3 eggs, separated
Seasoning

Oven temperature:	220°C/425°F/No.7
Position in oven:	Centre
Time in oven:	30 minutes
Number of servings:	4

Method

1. Butter a 1 litre (2 pint) soufflé or ovenproof dish.
2. Melt butter in pan, stir in flour, gradually add milk and bring sauce to boil, stirring all the time.

3. Remove pan from heat and add cheese, parsley and seasoning. Beat in egg yolks.
4. Whisk egg whites until stiff and gently fold into sauce mixture with a metal spoon.
5. Pour mixture into prepared dish and bake for about 30 mins. Serve immediately.

Note: It is vital not to open the door while the souffle is baking or it will fall.

Sandwiches

When making sandwiches, provide variety by using different types of bread and rolls, e.g. white, brown, rye, wheaten, vienna, french stick, etc.
Make sure that the butter, which should be soft, completely covers the bread. It acts as a barrier between the filling and bread, thus preventing the filling from making the bread soggy. Check seasoning of filling before making up sandwiches.
If using a soft filling, e.g. egg mayonnaise, use crisp lettuce leaves or chopped celery, to go with it as contrasting textures add interest. The lettuce leaves also provide an additional barrier between the soft filling and bread. This is particularly useful with open sandwiches which often use moist ingredients.

Some ideas for sandwich fillings:
Corned beef and chutney/tomato/tomato sauce or salad
Gammon and pineapple/tomato/mustard/salad/beetroot or peach chutney
Roast beef and horseradish sauce or salad
Turkey and cranberry sauce
Lamb and mint sauce
Pork and apple sauce
Chicken and salad or cucumber
Tuna fish and salad/onions/mayonnaise or cucumber
Salmon, lemon juice and salad
Sardines and tomato
Cheddar cheese and beetroot/chutney/pineapple/onion/tomato/salad/prawns/tuna fish or peanut butter
Cottage cheese and pineapple/chives/tuna fish/cucumber/prawns/walnuts or grated carrot
Egg and mayonnaise/tomato or cress
Pâté and tomato/cucumber or salad
Dates, lemon juice and walnuts

Farmhouse Pie

Ingredients
225g (8 oz) shortcrust pastry (see Step-by-Step Cookery p. 118)
50g (2 oz) Scottish cheddar cheese, finely grated
$\frac{1}{4}$ teaspoon nutmeg
Seasoning
225g (8 oz) smooth cottage cheese
3 small eggs
Milk to glaze

Oven temperature: 220°C/425°F/No.7
Position in oven: Centre
Time in oven: 40 minutes
Number of servings: 4

Method
1. Butter 18cm (7 inch) fluted flan dish or deep pie plate and line with half the pastry.
2. Mix the grated cheddar, nutmeg and seasoning into the smooth cottage cheese. Spread this over the pastry.
3. Make hollows in the cheese mixture and into these break the eggs. Season lightly. Cover with remaining pastry.
4. Stand dish on a baking tray, brush top with a little milk and bake in a hot oven for 40 minutes.

Desserts

Mocha Meringue Surprise

Ingredients
Meringue:

4 egg whites
225g (8 oz) caster sugar
½ teaspoon ground almonds

Filling:

½ teaspoon instant coffee
1 tablespoon soft dark brown sugar
280ml (½ pint) double cream
3 dessert pears
Hazelnuts to decorate

Oven temperature: 140°C/275°F/No. 1
Position in oven: Below centre
Time in oven: 1 hour
Number of servings: 6

Method

1. Whisk egg whites until stiff; add one tablespoon of measured caster sugar and continue beating for about 30 seconds. Sift the remaining sugar and fold into the egg whites with the ground almonds.
2. Pipe 2 × 20cm (8 in) rounds or spread on two baking sheets. Bake in oven for about 1 hour, until meringue has dried out.
3. Peel, halve and core pears, then poach them gently in 25g (1 oz) sugar and 140ml (¼ pint) water.
4. In a bowl, mix the coffee and brown sugar with one tablespoon of hot water and allow to cool.
5. Whip the cream, and as it begins to thicken, add the coffee mixture and continue to beat until thick.
6. Sandwich the two meringue rounds with the coffee cream mixture but reserve some for decoration.
7. Decorate the top with pear halves, swirls of coffee cream mixture and hazelnuts.

Syllabub

Ingredients

2 tablespoons lemon juice
2 level teaspoons lemon rind, finely grated
140ml (¼ pint) sherry
2 tablespoons brandy
50g (2 oz) caster sugar
280ml (½ pint) double cream
Pinch ground nutmeg

Pots au Heather Cream

Ingredients

75g (3 oz) plain chocolate
25g (1 oz) Scottish butter
3 eggs, separated
1 tablespoon Heather Cream liqueur
140ml (¼ pint) double cream, whipped

Number of servings: 4

Method

1. Break up chocolate and put in a bowl standing over a saucepan of hot water. Add butter and leave until both have melted, stirring once or twice.
2. Beat in egg yolks. When mixture is smooth remove from heat and stir in Heather Cream liqueur.
3. Beat egg whites until stiff and gently fold into chocolate mixture.
4. Pour into 4 individual dishes or sundae glasses and chill.
5. Serve decorated with whipped cream.

Number of servings: 4-6

Method

1. Put sherry, brandy, lemon juice, rind and sugar in a bowl. Leave for a minimum of 3 hours.
2. Add cream and nutmeg and whisk mixture until it thickens and forms soft peaks.
3. Transfer into individual glasses. Leave in a cool place for several hours before serving. Decorate with a little lemon peel, serve each with a brandy snap, shortbread or sponge fingers.

Brandy Baskets

Ingredients
50g (2 oz) Scottish butter
50g (2 oz) sugar
2 level tablespoons golden syrup
50g (2 oz) plain flour
$\frac{1}{2}$ teaspoon ground ginger
2 teaspoons lemon juice
140ml ($\frac{1}{4}$ pint) double cream, whipped
Fruit to decorate

Oven temperature:	170°C/325°F/No. 3
Position in oven:	Centre
Time in oven:	8 minutes
Makes approx:	28 baskets

Method

1. Put butter, sugar and syrup into pan. Stand over a low heat until melted.
2. Sift together flour and ginger. Add to melted mixture with lemon juice.
3. Drop 4 teaspoons of mixture (well apart to allow for spreading) onto a large buttered baking tray. Bake for approx. 8 minutes.

4. Leave 1 minute. Lift off with a palette knife. Quickly lay over the base of a cup and shape into a basket. Leave until firm and slide off cup. Repeat with rest of mixture.
5. When cold, fill baskets with whipped cream and decorate with fruit.

Christmas Torte

Ingredients
Pastry:
100g (4 oz) flour
50g (2 oz) Scottish butter
25g (1 oz) caster sugar
25g (1 oz) ground almonds
Pinch salt
1 egg, beaten

Filling:
225g (8 oz) mincemeat

Sponge:
50g (2 oz) Scottish butter
50g (2 oz) caster sugar
25g (1 oz) flour
1 egg, beaten
40g ($1\frac{1}{2}$ oz) ground almonds
Almond essence

Topping:
280ml ($\frac{1}{2}$ pint) double cream

Oven temperature:	200°C/400°F/No. 6
Position in oven:	Centre
Time in oven:	25-30 minutes
Number of servings:	6

Pastry Method

1. Sieve the flour and salt. Lightly rub in butter to a sandy texture.
2. Mix together sugar and egg. Make well in centre of flour and add sugar and egg mixture. Sprinkle ground almonds over the flour.
3. Work these ingredients together into a dough.
4. Roll out on floured board and line an 18cm (7 in) flan ring. Prick bottom with fork then spread with mincemeat.

Sponge Method

1. Cream butter and sugar together.
2. Add egg, sieved flour and almonds and 2-3 drops of essence. Mix well.
3. Spread sponge mixture on top of mincemeat and bake for 25-30 mins. Allow to cool.
4. Whip cream and spread $\frac{2}{3}$ of it on top of sponge. Cover sides with cream, then pipe the remainder as decoration on top.

Muscat Brulée

Ingredients

225g (8 oz) green grapes
225g (8 oz) black grapes
280ml (½ pint) double cream
75g (3 oz) brown sugar
3 tablespoons sherry, optional

Number of servings: 4

Method

1. Cut grapes in half and remove seeds. Place in an ovenproof dish, then pour the sherry over the grapes.
2. Whip cream and spread over grapes. Refrigerate overnight.
3. Cover thickly with brown sugar and cook under a pre-heated grill until sugar melts.
4. Serve immediately with grapes and cream icy cold and the sugar forming a hot crispy toffee topping.

Boozy Bread & Butter Pudding

Ingredients

6 slices bread
75g (3 oz) Scottish butter
50g (2 oz) sultanas
1 glass sherry
1 × 425g (15 oz) tin peach slices
3 eggs
560ml (1 pint) milk

Oven temperature: 190°C/375°F/No. 5
Position in oven: Centre
Time in oven: 1 hour
Number of servings: 4

Method

1. Butter the bread and use half of it to line the bottom of 1 litre (2 pint) ovenproof dish.
2. Soak the sultanas in the sherry for 15 minutes.
3. Strain the juice from the tinned fruit and pour half of it over the bread in the dish. Arrange the fruit on top.
4. Strain the sultanas, reserving the sherry and sprinkle them over the fruit. Cut the remaining slices of bread into small triangles and place on top of the fruit.
5. Beat the eggs together and add the milk. Mix in the sherry and pour over the pudding and leave to stand for ½ hour.
6. Bake in oven until set and golden brown.

Baked Lemon Rice

Ingredients

40g (1½ oz) pudding rice
560ml (1 pint) milk
25g (1 oz) sugar
Grated rind of ½ lemon
Little grated cinnamon

Oven temperature: 150°C/300°F/No. 2
Position in oven: Centre
Time in oven: 3 hours
Number of servings: 4

Method

1. Wash the rice, and put into a greased 1 litre (2 pint) ovenproof dish.
2. Add the sugar, grated lemon rind and milk to dish.
3. Shake cinnamon on top, then bake in oven for about 3 hours until creamy.
4. Serve with whipped cream and fruit, if desired. Decorate with lemon.

Strawberry Flan

Ingredients

1 cooked 20cm (8 in) sponge or pastry flan case

sauce:
25g (1 oz) Scottish butter
25g (1 oz) cornflour
140ml (¼ pint) milk
25g (1 oz) caster sugar
1 egg yolk
1 tablespoon double cream
1 tablespoon Cointreau

225g (8 oz) fresh strawberries

glaze:
1 level teaspoon arrowroot
140ml (¼ pint) water
25g (1 oz) sugar

140ml (¼ pint) double cream

Number of servings: 4-6

Method

1. Place butter, cornflour and milk in a pan and heat, stirring continuously until sauce thickens and boils.
2. Stir in sugar, egg yolk, double cream and Cointreau, then spread in flan case.
3. Halve the strawberries and arrange them over the filling.
4. Blend arrowroot with a little of the water. Boil the remaining water with the sugar to make a syrup. Add arrowroot mixture and bring to the boil to thicken. Cool slightly then brush over the strawberries.
5. Decorate with whipped cream.

N.B. The arrowroot glaze can be replaced by piping jelly and when in a hurry, replace the fruit and glaze with a tin of pie filling.

Gowrie Tipple

Ingredients
280ml ($\frac{1}{2}$ pint) double cream
225g (8 oz) fresh raspberries
Drambuie to taste
Flaked almonds, toasted

Number of servings: 4

Method

1. Lightly whip cream and add Drambuie to taste.
2. Layer cream and raspberries alternately into individual sundae glasses.
3. Decorate with toasted flaked almonds.

Yogurt Sponge Cake

Ingredients

100g (4 oz) Scottish butter
100g (4 oz) caster sugar
1 large egg
150g (6 oz) self raising flour
2 × 125g (5 oz) cartons hazelnut yogurt
2 tablespoons cocoa powder
3 tablespoons milk
75g (3 oz) desiccated coconut

Oven temperature:	180°C/350°F/No. 4
Position in oven:	centre
Time in oven:	50 minutes
Number of servings:	4

Method

1. Grease a 1 litre (2 pint) ovenproof dish.
2. Cream the butter and sugar.
3. Beat egg and add with one carton of yogurt to creamed mixture.
4. Sieve flour and fold in.
5. Turn mixture into prepared dish and spread

evenly. Bake in oven until golden brown.
6. Meanwhile blend the cocoa with the milk and add remaining carton of yogurt. Stir in coconut.
7. Spread cocoa mixture evenly over the cooked sponge and place under a pre-heated grill for 2-3 minutes to set.
8. Sprinkle with caster sugar and serve hot with custard or cream.

N.B. The cake may also be left in the dish until cold and turned out. This is an unusual mixture of sweet and sour flavours and can be served as a special occasion gateau decorated with rosettes of whipped cream.

Baked Rum'n'Raisin Cheesecake

Ingredients

100g (4 oz) shortcrust pastry (see Step by Step Cookery p. 118)
3 eggs, separated
20g (¾ oz) flour
75g (3 oz) caster sugar
70ml (⅛ pint) soured cream
140ml (¼ pint) double cream
225g (8 oz) smooth cottage cheese
2 tablespoons dark rum
50g (2 oz) raisins
Icing sugar, to decorate

Oven temperature:	200°C/400°F/No. 6
Position in oven:	Centre
Time in oven:	50-60 minutes
Number of servings:	4-6

Method

1. Roll out pastry and use to line the base of a 20cm (8 in) loose-bottomed cake tin. Prick lightly with a fork and bake at 200°C/400°F/No. 6 for 5-10 minutes.
2. Whisk the egg yolks with the flour and sugar until smooth. Mix in soured cream and double cream.
3. Soak the raisins in rum for 15 minutes.
4. Gradually blend the soured cream mixture into the smooth cottage cheese.
5. Whisk the egg whites stiffly and fold into the mixture with the rum and raisins. Pour the mixture into tin and bake at 170°C/325°F/No. 3 for 45-50 minutes until firm.
6. Allow to cool in the tin then remove and dredge with icing sugar.

Butterscotch Flan

Ingredients:
100g (4 oz) shortcrust pastry (see Step by Step cookery p 118)

Filling:
150g (6 oz) soft dark brown sugar
3 tablespoons cornflour
560ml (1 pint) milk
2 eggs
50g (2 oz) Scottish butter
½ teaspoon vanilla essence
25g (1 oz) flaked almonds, toasted
140ml (¼ pint) double cream, whipped

Oven temperature:	190°C/375°F/No. 5
Position in oven:	Centre
Time in oven:	20 minutes
Number of servings:	4-6

Method
1. Roll out pastry and line a 18cm (7 in) fluted flan dish. Bake "blind" in a fairly hot oven for about 20 mins.
2. To make butterscotch filling, mix cornflour to a smooth paste with a little of the cold milk.
3. Pour rest of milk into pan, add butter and sugar. Stand over a low heat and stir until sugar dissolves.
4. Beat eggs lightly in a bowl and add cornflour paste to bowl. Add a little of the hot mixture to bowl and mix well, blend with remaining hot milk mixture. Cook, stirring continuously until mixture thickens. Add vanilla essence and simmer for 3 minutes, stirring all the time. Allow to cool.
5. Fill cooked pastry case with butterscotch filling and leave until set.
6. When ready to serve, decorate with whipped cream and sprinkle with toasted flaked almonds.

Heather Cream Fondue

Ingredients
225g (8 oz) milk chocolate
1 tablespoon instant coffee powder
140ml (¼ pint) double cream
2 tablespoons Heather Cream liqueur

Number of servings: 4

Method
1. Grate chocolate and mix with instant coffee powder.
2. Place cream in fondue pot, add chocolate and coffee. Heat gently stirring continuously until chocolate has melted.
3. Stir in Heather Cream liqueur. Serve hot with a selection of biscuits, plain cake, sponge fingers, marshmallows, turkish delight or pieces of fruit for dipping in the fondue.

Kiwi Caprice

Ingredients
4 kiwi fruits
140ml (¼ pint) double cream
2 large meringue shells

Number of servings: 4

Method
1. Peel and chop 3 of the kiwi fruit.
2. Whip cream lightly and mix in chopped fruit.
3. Crush meringues and add to cream and frui mixture.
4. Place cream mixture into 4 individual glasses.
5. Peel and slice remaining kiwi fruit. Decorate glasses with slices of kiwi fruit.

HEATHER CREAM
CREAM & SCOTCH MALT WHISKY
CREAM LIQUEUR
70cl
1 1/4 OZ.

Mandarin Yogurt Cheesecake

Ingredients
Base:

100g (4 oz) digestive biscuits, crushed
50g (2 oz) Scottish butter

Filling:

1 × 125g (5 oz) carton mandarin yogurt
100g (4 oz) smooth cottage cheese
50g (2 oz) caster sugar
140ml ($\frac{1}{4}$ pint) double cream

Mandarins to decorate

Number of servings: 4-6

Method

1. To make base — melt butter, add biscuit crumbs and press into a 20cm (8 in) loose bottomed cake tin. Chill.
2. To make filling — whip cream until stiff.

Mix half the cream with the yogurt, cottage cheese and sugar until smooth.
3. Spoon the mixture over the base and chill until firm. Decorate with remaining cream and mandarins.

Note: Any flavoured yogurt and fruit can be used; e.g. strawberry, raspberry, lemon or even hazelnut.

Pineapple Crunch

Ingredients
1 × 250g (9 oz) tin crushed pineapple, drained
$\frac{1}{2}$ teaspoon ground ginger (optional)
1 egg
2 tablespoons cornflour
1 tablespoon golden syrup
280ml ($\frac{1}{2}$ pint) milk
40g (1$\frac{1}{2}$ oz) Scottish butter
3 shredded wheat biscuits or
75g (3 oz) rolled oats
40g (1$\frac{1}{2}$ oz) brown sugar

Oven temperature: 180°C/350°F/No. 4
Position in oven: centre
Time in oven: 15 minutes
Number of servings: 4

Method

1. Place drained pineapple in a $\frac{3}{4}$ litre (1 pint) ovenproof dish or 4 individual ovenproof dishes and sprinkle with ground ginger.
2. Beat egg, cornflour and syrup together. Stir

in milk then place in pan and cook over a low heat, whisking continuously, until thickened. Cool slightly and pour over the pineapple.
3. Melt butter in a pan, stir in the crushed shredded wheat (or rolled oats) and sugar. Sprinkle over the custard and bake in oven.
4. Serve immediately.

NB: This dessert can also be served cold, layered in glasses. 450g (1 lb) cooked rhubarb can be substituted in place of crushed pineapple.

Rhubarb Hotcake

Ingredients
225g (8 oz) self-raising flour
Pinch salt
25g (1 oz) Scottish butter
25g (1 oz) caster sugar
1 egg, beaten
140ml ($\frac{1}{4}$ pint) milk

Filling:
225g (8 oz) rhubarb, trimmed and chopped
50g (2 oz) caster sugar
Knob of Scottish butter

Icing sugar

Oven temperature:	190°C/375°F/No. 5
Position in oven:	Centre
Time in oven:	40 minutes
Number of servings:	8

Method
1. Rub butter into flour until the fine breadcrumb stage, then add the sugar.

2. Mix the egg into a little milk, add to mixture and finally add as much extra milk as is necessary to make a soft dough.
3. Divide into half and roll into 2 × 18 cm (7 in) rounds on a lightly floured board.
4. Put first round on a lightly greased baking sheet, cover with chopped rhubarb mixed with sugar, dot with butter.
5. Cut second round into eight wedges and place on top of rhubarb. Bake for about 40 minutes.
6. Serve hot, dusted with icing sugar. Accompany with custard, or single cream.

Hot Swiss Trifle

Ingredients
1 swiss roll
1 × 425g (15 oz) tin apricots, drained
2 tablespoons custard powder
2 eggs, separated
1 tablespoon sugar
560ml (1 pint) milk
100g (4 oz) caster sugar

Oven temperature:	180°C/350°F/No. 4
Position in oven:	Centre
Time in oven:	20 minutes
Number of servings:	4-6

Method
1. Slice the swiss roll and arrange with the apricots in a 1 litre (2 pint) heatproof dish.
2. Blend the custard powder, egg yolks and sugar together with a little of the milk.
3. Heat remaining milk and when nearly boiling, stir on to the mixed custard.
4. Return to the pan and bring to the boil, stirring continuously. When thick, pour over

apricots.
5. Whisk the egg whites until stiff and fold in caster sugar.
6. Pile the meringue on top of the custard. Bake in a moderate oven for about 20 minutes.

N.B. Any tinned fruit may be substituted for the apricots used in this recipe.

Lemon Cheesecake

Ingredients
Base:

150g (6 oz) wheatmeal biscuits
25g (1 oz) caster sugar
50g (2 oz) Scottish butter, melted

Filling:

225g (8 oz) smooth cottage cheese
100g (4 oz) lemon curd
3 egg yolks

Oven temperature: 180°C/350°F/No. 4
Position in oven: Centre
Time in oven: 20 minutes
Number of servings: 6

Method

1. Crush the biscuits with a rolling pin in a polythene bag and mix with the sugar.
2. Mix $\frac{2}{3}$ of this into the melted butter and press into a 20cm (8 in) loose bottomed cake tin. Chill well.
3. Blend the cottage cheese and lemon curd together. Mix in the egg yolks. Pour the mixture into the chilled biscuit base.
4. Sprinkle the remaining biscuit crumbs over the filling, then bake for 20 minutes.
5. Cool and chill again before serving.

Pear & Lemon Surprise

Ingredients
420ml ($\frac{3}{4}$ pint) milk
25g (1 oz) Scottish butter
Grated rind of $\frac{1}{2}$ lemon
2 eggs, separated
25g (1 oz) granulated sugar
65g ($2\frac{1}{2}$ oz) fresh white breadcrumbs
3 tablespoons lemon curd
1 × 425g (15 oz) tin pear halves, drained
25g (1 oz) caster sugar

Oven Temperature: 180°C/350°F/No. 4
Position in oven: Centre
Time in oven: 40-50 minutes
Number of servings: 4-6

Method

1. Warm milk in a pan with butter and lemon rind. Beat the egg yolks with the granulated sugar, then stir into the warm milk.

2. Put breadcrumbs into a buttered 1 litre (2 pint) ovenproof dish. Strain milk mixture over this and allow to stand for 15 minutes then bake in a moderate oven for 25-30 minutes until lightly set.
3. Spread the lemon curd over the pudding, then place the pear halves on top.
4. Whisk the egg whites stiffly and fold in the caster sugar. Spread or pipe the meringue on top of the pears and bake for a further 15-20 minutes. Serve immediately.

Christmas Crunch Pears

Ingredients
50g (2 oz) Scottish butter
50g (2 oz) soft brown sugar
100g (4 oz) fresh white breadcrumbs
50g (2 oz) walnuts, chopped
Pinch cinnamon
4 dessertspoons mincemeat
4 fresh pears, peeled, halved and cored

Oven temperature: 180°C/350°F/No. 4
Position in oven: Centre
Time in oven: 45 minutes
Number of servings: 4

Method

1. Melt butter in pan, add sugar, breadcrumbs, walnuts and cinnamon.
2. Place pear halves in base of an ovenproof dish.
3. Fill each pear half with a spoonful of

mincemeat and cover with breadcrumb topping.

4. Bake in oven for 45 minutes and serve with whipped cream.

Dairy Ice Cream

Ingredients

4 eggs, separated
100g (4 oz) icing sugar, sieved
280ml (½ pint) double cream
¼ teaspoon vanilla essence

Number of servings: 6

Method

1. Set refrigerator to freezing.
2. Whisk egg yolks until light and creamy. Whisk whites until stiff, then gradually whisk in sugar. Whip up cream.
3. Add vanilla essence to yolks, fold in egg whites then whipped cream.
4. Turn into freezer tray and freeze for 1 hour. Stir well with a fork and refreeze for 2-3 hours.

Note: Instead of vanilla the following flavourings may be substituted:—
3 tablespoons coffee essence
100g (4 oz) grated chocolate
225g (8 oz) puréed fruit

Peach Melba Cheesecake

Ingredients
Base:

100g (4 oz) digestive biscuits, crushed
50g (2 oz) Scottish butter
Pinch cinnamon

Filling:

1 large peach, peeled, halved and stoned
225g (8 oz) smooth cottage cheese
75g (3 oz) icing sugar
1 egg
½ teaspoon almond essence
70ml (⅛ pint) soured cream

Topping:

100g (4 oz) fresh raspberries
25g (1 oz) caster sugar

Oven temperature:	180°C/350°F/No. 4
Position in oven:	Centre
Time in oven:	15-20 minutes
Number of servings:	6

Method

1. To make base — melt butter, add biscuit crumbs and cinnamon, mix well. Press into bottom of a 20cm (8 in) loose bottomed cake tin.
2. Slice the peach and arrange on the base.
3. To make filling — put cottage cheese in a bowl and blend in icing sugar, soured cream, egg and essence.
4. Pour mixture over the peach slices. Bake for 15-20 mins. or until set.
5. To make topping — rub the raspberries through a fine sieve into a bowl. Sweeten the resulting purée with the sugar.
6. Chill cheesecake for several hours or overnight before covering with the topping. Decorate with cream.

Baking

Chocolate Eclairs

Ingredients
Choux Pastry
190ml (7 fl. oz) water
50g (2 oz) Scottish butter
100g (4 oz) plain flour
3-4 eggs
Pinch salt
Pinch sugar
280ml (½ pint) double cream, whipped
75g (3 oz) cooking chocolate

Oven temperature: 200°C/400°F/No. 6
Position in oven: Centre
Time in oven: 30-35 minutes
Makes 12 eclairs

Method

1. Bring water, salt, butter and sugar to the boil in a pan.
2. Add flour and beat with a wooden spoon until the mixture leaves the sides of the pan.
3. Allow to cool slightly and beat in the eggs, one by one. Beat well until the mixture is smooth, shiny and firm enough to stand in soft peaks when lifted with the spoon.
4. Fit a piping bag with 1cm (½ in) plain tube and fill with choux paste.
5. Pipe twelve 10cm (4 in) lengths onto a buttered baking tray. Bake in oven at above temp. for 10 minutes then reduce to 180°C/350°F/No. 4 for a further 20-25 minutes (or until the eclairs are well puffed and golden).
6. Remove from oven and make a small slit in the side of each eclair, then return to oven for a further 5 minutes to dry out. Cool on a wire rack.
7. When completely cold, slit each eclair along one side. Melt chocolate in a bowl, over hot water and coat the tops of the eclairs by dipping them in the chocolate.
8. Finally, fill the eclairs with whipped cream. In the summer, eclairs filled with fresh fruit salad and served with fresh dairy cream are simply delicious.

Quickie Cream Cakes

Ingredients
1 chocolate swiss roll
140ml (¼ pint) double cream, whipped
Mandarin oranges
1 pkt. chocolate buttons

Makes: 6

Method

1. Cut swiss roll into 6 slices.
2. Pipe cream onto slices of swiss roll.
3. Decorate with mandarin oranges and chocolate buttons.

Note: Other fruits can be used, also cherries, nuts and angelica.

White Fruit Cake

Ingredients
100g (4 oz) glacé pineapple
150g (6 oz) red glacé cherries
150g (6 oz) green glacé cherries
100g (4 oz) crystallised ginger
100g (4 oz) sultanas
100g (4 oz) candied peel
3 tablespoons brandy
250g (9 oz) Scottish butter
250g (9 oz) caster sugar
4 large eggs
340g (12 oz) plain flour sieved
100g (4 oz) walnuts, chopped

Oven temperature: 150°C/300°F/No. 2
Position in oven: Below centre
Time in oven: 2¾ hours

Method

1. Wash sugar coating from cherries, pineapple and ginger in warm water and then pat dry.
2. Cut the cherries in half and coarsely chop the pineapple and ginger. Put in a bowl with sultanas and peel. Add brandy and leave to soak overnight.
3. Cream butter and sugar together until light and fluffy.
4. Lightly mix eggs and then gradually beat into the creamed mixture a little at a time, adding some of the flour with the last few additions of egg.
5. Using a metal spoon fold in the remaining flour and then the soaked fruit, with any liquid in the basin. Finally add the chopped walnuts.
6. Spoon the mixture into a greased and lined 20cm (8 in) cake tin, level the mixture and then hollow out the centre slightly. Bake for approx. 2¾ hours and allow cake to cool in the tin.

Pineapple Nut Loaf

Ingredients

75g (3 oz) Scottish butter
225g (8 oz) caster sugar
1 egg, beaten
1 × 150g (6 oz) tin crushed pineapple, drained
1 × 250g (9 oz) tin evaporated milk
1 tablespoon lemon juice
25g (1 oz) walnuts, chopped
340g (12 oz) plain flour
4 teaspoons baking powder
½ teaspoon bicarbonate of soda
1 teaspoon salt
½ teaspoon cinnamon

Oven temperature: 190°C/375°F/No. 5
Position in oven: Centre
Time in oven: 1-1¼ hours

Method

1. Cream the butter and sugar together in a bowl until light and fluffy.
2. Gradually beat in the egg, then add the crushed pineapple, evaporated milk, lemon juice and walnuts. Mix well.
3. Sieve the remaining ingredients and fold into the pineapple mixture.
4. Pour into a greased and lined 1kg (2 lb) loaf tin and bake in oven.
5. Allow to cool in the tin before turning out onto a wire rack.

Old Fashioned Spice Cake

Ingredients

100g (4 oz) Scottish butter
100g (4 oz) soft brown sugar
75g (3 oz) golden syrup
3 eggs, beaten
250g (9 oz) self-raising flour
140ml (¼ pint) buttermilk

Oven temperature: 180°C/350°F/No. 4
Position in oven: Centre
Time in oven: 70 minutes

Method

1. Line and grease a deep 20cm (8 in) cake tin.
2. Cream butter and sugar together until light and fluffy.
3. Beat in syrup and eggs, a little at a time.
4. Fold in flour and buttermilk alternately.
5. Pour into prepared tin and bake for about 70 minutes. Turn out and cool.

Cheese Scones

Ingredients

225g (8 oz) self-raising flour
1 teaspoon salt
1 teaspoon baking powder
25g (1 oz) Scottish butter
100g (4 oz) Scottish cheddar cheese, grated
1 egg and milk mixed together to make 140ml (¼ pint)

Oven temperature: 230°C/450°F/No. 8
Position in oven: Centre
Time in oven: 10 minutes

Method

1. Sieve all dry ingredients together then rub in butter.
2. Mix in cheese then add egg and milk. Mix thoroughly to form a fairly soft dough.
3. Roll out scone dough into a round 1cm (½ in) thick and cut out rounds using cutter.
4. Sprinkle tops of scones with a little grated cheese. Place on a floured baking tray and bake in oven until golden brown and firm.

Madeira Cake

Ingredients

100g (4 oz) Scottish butter
100g (4 oz) caster sugar
2 eggs, beaten
225g (8 oz) plain flour
2 level teaspoons baking powder
3-4 tablespoons milk
½ teaspoon grated lemon rind

Oven temperature: 180°C/350°F/No. 4
Position in oven: below centre
Time in oven: 1-1¼ hours

Method

1. Line the sides and bottom of a deep cake tin 15cm (6 in) diameter with greaseproof paper.
2. Cream butter and sugar until light and fluffy. Add beaten eggs and milk gradually.
3. Stir in sieved flour and baking powder. Add lemon rind.
4. Put mixture into prepared cake tin and bake in moderate oven.

Cherry Cake

Use the above recipe but substitute 100g (4 oz) glacé cherries for the lemon rind. The cherries should be washed and dried and cut up roughly.

Sultana Cake

Use the above recipe but substitute 225g-275g (8-10 oz) sultanas for the lemon rind.

Fruit Loaf

Ingredients

100g (4 oz) Scottish butter
140ml (¼ pint) water
100g (4 oz) raisins
100g (4 oz) sultanas
225g (8 oz) self-raising flour
100g (4 oz) caster sugar
2 eggs, beaten
2 teaspoons bicarbonate of soda

Oven temperature: 180°C/350°F/No. 4
Position in oven: Centre
Time in oven: 45-60 minutes

Method

1. Melt butter in pan. Add water, raisins and sultanas, boil for five minutes.
2. Mix in the flour, sugar, eggs and bicarbonate of soda.
3. Place in a greased 1kg (2 lb) loaf tin and bake in a moderate oven for 45 minutes then reduce heat to 150°C/300°F/No. 2 for 15 minutes.

Quick Yogurt Cake

Ingredients

1 × 125g (5 oz) carton natural or hazelnut yogurt
2 × yogurt carton full of self-raising flour
1½ × yogurt carton of sugar
¼ × yogurt carton of melted Scottish butter
2 eggs
1 lemon, grated rind and juice } icing
Icing sugar }

Oven temperature: 180°C/350°F/No. 4
Position in oven: Centre
Time in oven: 45 minutes

Method

1. Put all ingredients in a bowl and mix well.
2. Pour mixture into a greased 18cm (7 in) sandwich tin and bake, until golden brown.
3. When cool, heat lemon juice in pan. Stir in sifted icing sugar and make a thick smooth consistency. Spread over cooled cake and leave to set.

Chocolate Tiffin

Ingredients

225g (8 oz) digestive biscuits, crushed
50g (2 oz) glacé cherries, chopped
100g (4 oz) Scottish butter
3 level tablespoons syrup
25g (1 oz) drinking chocolate
150g (6 oz) cooking chocolate for top

Method

1. Line a swiss roll tin with cling film.
2. Melt butter and syrup in a pan. Add drinking chocolate, biscuits and cherries and mix well.
3. Place mixture in prepared tin, press down well, leave until cold.
4. Melt the chocolate in a bowl over boiling water and pour over mixture spreading evenly.
5. When set, pull out tiffin with cling film and cut into required size.

Oatmeal Biscuits

Ingredients

100g (4 oz) porridge oats
100g (4 oz) Scottish butter
50g (2 oz) caster sugar
50g (2 oz) self-raising flour

Oven temperature: 170°C/325°F/No. 3
Position in oven: Centre
Time in oven: 20 minutes
Makes 16 biscuits

Method

1. Cream butter and sugar then add porridge oats and flour.
2. Roll into small balls and flatten slightly. Place on a greased baking tray and bake in a moderate oven.

Butter Shortbread

Ingredients
150g (6 oz) plain flour
Pinch salt
100g (4 oz) Scottish butter
50g (2 oz) caster sugar

Oven temperature: 170°C/325°F/No. 3
Position in oven: Centre
Time in oven: 40 minutes

Method
1. Add salt to flour.
2. Cream butter and sugar well.
3. Gradually work the flour into creamed mixture and knead until smooth.
4. Form mixture into a round or oblong shape about 1cm ($\frac{1}{2}$ in) thick.
5. Place on a baking tray, prick and decorate edges with fork. Bake until golden brown.
6. Cut into required size of pieces when hot and sprinkle with caster sugar, then cool on a wire rack.

Highlanders Shortbread

Ingredients
Base:
1 × Butter Shortbread recipe (see above)

Filling:
1 × Heather Cream Sauce recipe (see page 42, Liqueur Sauces, No.6)

Topping:
150g (6 oz) plain cooking chocolate

Oven temperature: 170°C/325°F/No. 3
Position in oven: Centre
Time in oven: 20-25 minutes

Method
1. Make up one quantity of butter shortbread from the recipe above and press mixture into a swiss roll tin. Prick all over with a fork and bake.
2. Make up one quantity of Heather Cream sauce and pour it over the cooked shortbread base. Leave to cool.
3. Melt chocolate in a bowl over a pan of hot water and spread over the Heather Cream sauce. Allow chocolate to harden before cutting into fingers.

Nutty Noodles

Ingredients
Pastry:
100g (4 oz) plain flour
50g (2 oz) Scottish butter
25g (1 oz) caster sugar
Cold water to mix

Filling:
1 egg
50g (2 oz) walnuts, chopped
75g (3 oz) brown sugar
75g (3 oz) raisins
Few drops vanilla essence

Oven temperature: 170°C/325°F/No.3
Position in oven: Centre
Time in oven: 25-30 minutes
Makes: 18 cakes

Method
1. Make up shortcrust pastry by rubbing butter into flour until like fine breadcrumbs.
2. Mix in sugar then bind together with as little water as possible.

3. Roll out pastry thinly and line patty tins.
4. Make filling by beating together egg, brown sugar, walnuts, raisins and vanilla essence.
5. Place teaspoonfuls of filling in pastry cases and bake in a moderate oven.

Confectionery

Ingredients
100g (4 oz) plain chocolate
50g (2 oz) Scottish butter
3 tablespoons single cream
1 teaspoon vanilla essence
450g (1 lb) icing sugar, sieved

Makes 60 squares

Method
1. Break up chocolate, put with butter in a bowl standing over a pan of hot water and stir until melted.
2. Remove bowl from pan and stir in cream and vanilla. Gradually work in icing sugar and mix well.
3. Transfer to buttered 20cm (8 inch) square tin and leave to cool until firm and set. Cut to required size.

N.B. To give a mocha flavour to the fudge; add 4 level teaspoons instant coffee powder to the chocolate and butter in the bowl.

Ingredients
450g (1 lb) icing sugar, sieved
1 teaspoon peppermint essence
50g (2 oz) Scottish butter, melted
2 tablespoons milk
Extra sifted icing sugar

Makes 60

Method
1. Combine melted butter with milk and gradually stir into sieved icing sugar.
2. Add peppermint essence and mix well.
3. Turn out onto a surface dusted with sifted icing sugar. Roll out to about $\frac{1}{4}$cm ($\frac{1}{8}$ inch) thickness. Score surface of mixture with a fork.
4. Cut about 60 rounds with $3\frac{1}{2}$cm ($1\frac{1}{4}$ inch) plain biscuit cutter. Leave in a cool place until firm.

N.B. These peppermint creams are also delicious half dipped or dipped in chocolate.

Candle Cakes

Ingredients
25g (1 oz) Scottish butter
1 tablespoon lemon curd
$\frac{1}{4}$ teaspoon vanilla essence
1-2 tablespoons icing sugar
4 tablespoons desiccated coconut
Extra icing sugar
Extra desiccated coconut

Makes 6

Method
1. Beat butter, lemon curd and vanilla essence together in a bowl until soft.
2. Beat in coconut and sufficient icing sugar to give a stiff consistency.
3. Divide coconut mixture into 6 equal pieces and roll each into a ball on a surface sprinkled with icing sugar.
4. Make up a little water icing, using 1 tablespoon icing sugar and dip each coconut ball in the icing, before tossing in coconut.
5. Place each in a paper case and leave in a cool place until firm.

To decorate — Place a small red or yellow candle in each cake and sit one at each place setting for Christmas.

Coconut Tablet

Ingredients
875g (2 lbs) granulated sugar
100g (4 oz) coconut
210ml ($\frac{3}{8}$ pint) milk
25g (1 oz) Scottish butter
Colouring if desired

Method
1. Heat milk and sugar slowly until sugar has dissolved then add butter and coconut, stirring all the time.
2. Bring to boil and boil to 240°F or soft ball. (To test for this see Vanilla Tablet, p. 103)
3. Take off heat and beat until thick and beginning to grain.
4. Quickly pour half into a buttered tray, add a little red colouring to remainder, stir in well then pour over white tablet in tray.
5. When cool, mark into squares.

Heather Cream Truffles

Ingredients

100g (4 oz) plain chocolate
50g (2 oz) Scottish butter
50g (2 oz) ground almonds
225g (8 oz) icing sugar, sieved
1 tablespoon double cream
1 tablespoon strong black coffee
1 tablespoon Heather Cream Liqueur
Sieved drinking chocolate

Makes: 36

Method

1. Melt chocolate and butter in a bowl over a pan of hot water.
2. Add coffee and blend in with Heather Cream Liqueur and double cream.
3. Stir in ground almonds and icing sugar.
4. Leave to cool, then roll into small balls and toss in drinking chocolate. Place in small paper sweet cases and serve with after-dinner coffee.

Marzipan Sweets

Ingredients

450g (1 lb) marzipan
A variety of colourings

Method

1. Divide the marzipan into 4 portions. One by one flatten each portion and add the colouring. Knead each marzipan portion until it is evenly coloured, then shape them into balls. Dust a rolling pin with icing sugar and roll out one of the balls into a rectangle. Roll out the other balls in the same way. Stack the rectangles in layers; to make the surfaces stick together brush each rectangle with lightly beaten egg white. With a rolling pin, lightly roll over the top of the stack to press the layers together. To make a neat rectangular shape, trim away the uneven edges. With a long, sharp knife, cut the rectangle lengthwise into equal-sized strips. Slice the marzipan across at 1cm ($\frac{1}{2}$ inch) intervals. Leave them to dry uncovered, for a few hours or overnight. Serve the sweets piled on a dish.
2. Divide the marzipan into two portions, one twice the size of the other. Knead some colouring into the larger portion and divide it in two. Leave the rest uncoloured. With your palms, roll out one coloured portion into a long, thin sausage-shape. Roll the remaining portions out into narrow rectangles the length of the coloured sausage-shape. Brush the rectangles with egg white and place the coloured sausage-shape along one long edge of the uncoloured rectangle. Roll the rectangle around the sausage-shape. In the same way, roll the coloured rectangle around the sausage-shape and cut off any overlap. Trim the ends, then slice the roll at 1cm. ($\frac{1}{2}$ inch) intervals. When the marzipans have hardened and dried slightly, after 1 to 2 hours, pile into a dish and serve.

Stuffed Dates & Walnuts

Ingredients

450g (1 lb) dates, stoned
225g (8 oz) walnut halves
450g (1 lb) marzipan
5 tablespoons white rum
1 tablespoon strong black coffee
Green or pink colouring

Method

1. To stuff the dates, moisten half the marzipan with 3 tablespoons of the rum and a few drops of green or pink colouring. Roll a little marzipan into a ball and use it to fill the cavity left by the stone. Arrange them in paper cases and serve.
2. To stuff the walnuts, flavour the rest of the marzipan with 2 tablespoons of the rum and the black coffee. Roll a little marzipan into a ball and sandwich it between two walnut halves. Arrange them in paper cases and serve

VENUS
SATURN
SUN
AQUARIUS

Chocolate Clusters

Ingredients

125g (5 oz) chocolate
1 tablespoon raisins
1 tablespoon chopped nuts
Grated rind of 1 orange
1 tablespoon Grand Marnier

Method

1. Melt chocolate in a bowl over a pan of hot water.
2. Add raisins, chopped nuts, orange rind and Grand Marnier to the melted chocolate. Mix well.
3. Line a tray with wax paper. Remove teaspoonfuls of the chocolate mixture and with another teaspoon, push the spoonfuls of mixture on to the wax paper. Leave in a cool place until they have completely set, about 1 hour.
4. Place the sweets in paper cases to serve them.

N.B. If desired to give a smooth finish and extra chocolate flavour the sweets can be dipped in melted chocolate.

Vanilla Tablet

Ingredients

?75g (2 lbs) granulated sugar
?00g (4 oz) Scottish butter
? × 396g (14 oz) tin condensed milk
?40ml (¼ pint) milk
Little vanilla essence

Method

- Melt butter with milk in pan then add sugar.
- Dissolve sugar in mixture stirring all the time.
- Add condensed milk and bring mixture to boil still stirring constantly.
- Bring mixture to soft ball consistency 240°F (either use a sugar thermometer to test or drop a little mixture into a cup of cold water, leave for 1 minute and, if you can form a soft ball between finger and thumb, the tablet is ready).
- Take off heat, add essence and beat mixture until it begins to thicken and grain. Pour into a buttered tin and when set, mark into squares.

Quick Cream Truffles

Ingredients

140ml (¼ pint) double cream
275g (10 oz) milk chocolate, roughly chopped
1 tablespoon Cointreau
Ground almonds or chocolate vermicelli

Method

1. Heat cream in saucepan until boiling.
2. Remove pan from heat, add chopped chocolate and stir until melted. Add Cointreau.
3. Line a swiss roll tin with cling film and pour mixture into tin. Place in refrigerator until cold and firm — preferably overnight.
4. Remove mixture from tin and roll into small balls. Toss in ground almonds or chocolate vermicelli and serve in small paper sweet cases.

N.B. Any spirit or liqueur may be used to give special flavours. This type of truffle can be kept in a refrigerator for several weeks.

Milk Drinks & Cocktails

Chocolate Cream Cooler

Ingredients
1 glass cold milk
3 teaspoons drinking chocolate
1 tablespoon boiling water
1 tablespoon Heather Cream Liqueur

To decorate: whipped cream and grated chocolate

Number of servings: 1

Method
1. Mix drinking chocolate to a smooth consistency with water.
2. Whisk in milk and Heather Cream Liqueur.
3. Pour into a tall glass and top with whipped cream. Sprinkle with grated chocolate.

Capuccino

Ingredients
280ml ($\frac{1}{2}$ pint) milk
1 teaspoon instant coffee
Drinking chocolate

Number of servings: 2

Method
1. Heat milk and coffee powder in a saucepan.
2. Pour hot milk into liquidiser and liquidise for about 1-2 minutes.
3. Serve hot in a cup, sprinkled with drinking chocolate.

Rum Crunch

Ingredients
280ml ($\frac{1}{2}$ pint) cold milk
$\frac{1}{2}$ banana, mashed
1 tablespoon rum
Chopped walnuts

Number of servings: 1

Method
1. Whisk together milk, rum and mashed banana.
2. Pour into a tall glass and serve topped with chopped nuts.

Strawberry Freshener

Ingredients
1 × 125g (5 oz) carton strawberry yogurt
140ml ($\frac{1}{4}$ pint) chilled buttermilk

To decorate: a fresh strawberry

Number of servings: 1

Method
1. Whisk yogurt and buttermilk together.
2. Pour into a tall glass and serve topped with a fresh strawberry.

Ginger Slim

Ingredients
1 tablespoon lime milk shake syrup
140 ml ($\frac{1}{4}$ pint) cold milk
Ginger beer

Number of servings: 1

Method
1. Mix milk and lime syrup together.
2. Pour into a glass and top up with ginger beer.

Raspberry Frappé

Ingredients

1 tablespoon raspberry milk shake syrup
1 × 150g (6 oz) tin evaporated milk
140ml ($\frac{1}{4}$ pint) cold milk

To decorate: 1 scoop vanilla ice cream

Number of servings: 1

Method

1. Pour milk into a jug. Add milk shake syrup and evaporated milk.
2. Whisk until thoroughly blended. Pour into a tall glass and top with a scoop of ice cream.

Mocha Mallow Float

Ingredients

280ml ($\frac{1}{2}$ pint) milk
2 teaspoons drinking chocolate
1 teaspoon instant coffee powder
2 tablespoons Heather Cream Liqueur
1 or 2 marshmallows

Number of servings: 1

Method

1. Heat milk. Add drinking chocolate, coffee powder and Heather Cream Liqueur. Whisk thoroughly.
2. Pour into a mug and top with one or two marshmallows.

Ingredients

280ml ($\frac{1}{2}$ pint) milk
2 teaspoons golden syrup
Pinch cinnamon
Pinch mixed spice

Number of servings: 1

Method

1. Heat milk in a saucepan. Add syrup, cinnamon and mixed spice.
2. Serve hot in a mug or glass.

Hawaiian Crush

Ingredients

280ml ($\frac{1}{2}$ pint) cold milk
1 scoop dairy ice cream
2 pineapple rings, chopped

Number of servings: 1

Method

1. Place milk, ice cream and pineapple rings into a liquidiser. Liquidise for 1 minute.
2. Pour into a tall glass and serve chilled, garnished with fresh pineapple.

Gaelic Coffee

Ingredients

1 teaspoon brown sugar
2 tablespoons Scotch Whisky
1 cup strong black coffee
Lightly whipped double cream

Number of servings: 1

Method

1. Put sugar into a heat resistant glass.
2. Add whisky and black coffee. Stir well to dissolve sugar.
3. Pour lightly whipped cream over a spoon on top of coffee.

If you are not an expert at cake decoration, you are better to work within your skills and execute a design well and neatly, rather than tackle something which is very difficult and make a mess of it. As you get to know the types of icing and decoration you are using, you can advance as you feel more confident of your skills.

In the following pages you will find a variety of cakes at different levels of skills and for different occasions.

Butter Sponge

Ingredients

100g (4 oz) Scottish butter
100g (4 oz) caster sugar
2 standard eggs
150g (6 oz) self-raising flour, sieved
For Chocolate Sponge, add 2 tablespoons drinking chocolate along with flour
For Lemon Sponge, add the grated rind of one lemon.

Oven temperature: 190°C/375°F/No. 5
Position in oven: Centre
Time in oven: 25-30 minutes

Method

1. Butter two 18 cm (7 in) round sandwich tins.
2. Cream butter and sugar together until pale in colour, light in texture, and fluffy.
3. Beat in whole eggs, one at a time, adding one tablespoon of flour with each.
4. Gently fold in remaining flour with metal spoon.
5. Divide mixture into prepared tins and smooth tops with knife.
6. Bake in moderate oven until well risen, golden brown and firm.
7. Leave in tins 2-3 minutes. Turn out onto a cooling rack. When cold, fill and decorate with freshly whipped double cream and fruit. In the summer, raspberries and strawberries are delicious in this cream gâteau.

Strawberry Cream Gâteau

Ingredients

2 × 18 cm (7 in) egg sponges (Step by Step page 123)
280ml (½ pint) whipping cream
225g (8 oz) fresh strawberries

Method

The egg sponge should be made on the day it is to be eaten.

1. Hull and wash the strawberries and select about half of a uniform shape for the top.
2. Slice the rest of the strawberries.
3. Whip up cream until stiff and place two thirds into a piping bag with a number 8 star pipe in it.
4. Mix sliced strawberries and one third of cream together and sandwich sponges with this mixture.
5. Decorate top of gâteau with strawberries and cream.

2 × 18 cm (7 in) Lemon sponges (as recipe on this page)
Lemon curd as required
Flaked almonds
Lemon butter icing (as recipe on page 111)
Lemon jelly slices
Water icing, white and lemon

Method

1. Split sponges in half and sandwich all together with lemon curd.
2. Put butter icing round outside of cake and roll in almonds.
3. Make up sufficient white water icing for top of cake. Colour a small amount of icing yellow and place in piping bag.
4. Spread white icing on top and immediately put rows of yellow icing across cake. Take a skewer and drag skewer across icing .
5. Leave to dry and when dry, finish off top with butter icing and lemon jelly slices.

Ingredients

2 × 18cm (7 in) Chocolate butter sponges (as recipe on this page)
Little cooking chocolate
280ml (½ pint) double cream
1-2 tablespoons liqueur of your choice (suggestions: Cointreau, Heather Cream, Drambuie)

Method

1. Whip up cream and liqueur until thick.
2. Split sponges and sandwich the four rounds together with cream mixture.
3. Cover top and sides of gâteau with the rest of the cream and decorate using a star pipe and a little chocolate as photograph.

Cake Decoration

ALISON JANE
HAPPY BIRTHDAY
CAMPBELL
A Happy
Birthday

Birthday Cake House

The main part of the house is roughly 8″ across × 5″ deep, and on top of that goes a piece of cake a suitable size for the roof. Stick the roof onto the main part of the house with jam and then cover the whole house with marzipan. Cover the marzipan with butter icing and while wet, put tiles in place or flat sweets, whatever you are going to use for the tiles. The door is a chocolate bar and the windows are outlined either with chocolate sticks or butter icing. The garden fence is made from chocolate sticks and the grass is green sugar with a border of chocolate butter icing. Place flowers in the icing and if you can get little figures, put them into the garden. Candles are placed round the fence where they fit in and the name of the person whose birthday it is goes on a flag on the roof.

Birthday Cake Train

This can be made out of an 8″ square cake cut into four pieces of 3″ × 4″. This leaves a small piece of cake for the engine cab which is fixed with a little jam. Cover the engine and the trucks with marzipan and on the trucks place a ½″ × ¼″ line of marzipan round the top edge of each one. The funnel is marzipan. Dip each side of the truck and the engine in melted chocolate and leave to dry. Fill each truck with sweets. The wheels are put in place with a little butter icing. Candles can be put on the trucks and the child's name is put on a flag which flies from the funnel of the engine.

How to Marzipan a Cake

The sides of the cake are covered in marzipan first and this is done by rolling out a long thin strip of marzipan to fit. Spread apricot jam onto the marzipan and then place the edge of the cake on part of the marzipan and wrap the rest of it round the cake. You then roll out a piece of marzipan which will fit exactly onto the top of the cake and again, spread jam onto the marzipan and then place the cake on top of the marzipan. When you have done this, smooth the marzipan down as best you can with your hands. The cake should be left for a day before icing.

Coffee Gâteau

Ingredients

2 × 18cm (7 in) Butter sponges (as in page 108)
Coffee butter icing as recipe below.
100g (4 oz) chopped walnuts
50g (2 oz) whole walnuts

Method

1. Sandwich sponges together with icing and then spread sides with icing.
2. Roll sides of sponge in chopped walnuts.
3. Decorate top with remainder of icing and whole walnuts as photograph.

Butter Icing

Ingredients

100g (4 oz) Scottish butter
150g (6 oz) icing sugar, sieved
1-2 tablespoons milk
Little vanilla essence

Variations

Lemon – substitute lemon juice for milk and omit vanilla essence

Chocolate – omit vanilla and add 1 tablespoon cocoa powder

Coffee – omit vanilla and add 2-3 teaspoons instant coffee powder.

Method

1. Cream butter, then gradually add icing sugar a little at a time along with milk.
2. Add flavouring required.

Rich Fruit Cake

23cm (9 in) round or 20cm (8 in) square tin
Ingredients
390g (14 oz) flour
340g (12 oz) Scottish butter
340g (12 oz) soft brown sugar
6 eggs beaten
2 teaspoons cinnamon
1 teaspoon mixed spice
1.36kg (3 lbs) dried fruit made up from sultanas, raisins, currants, mixed peel and glace cherries

Oven temperature: 150°C/300°F/No. 2
Position in oven: lowest shelf
Time in oven: 4 hours

Method

1. Prepare tin by lining with greaseproof paper and greasing well with butter. Sieve flour and spices together.
2. Cream butter and sugar well, then add eggs and dry ingredients alternately. Mix in dried fruit.
3. Place in prepared tin and bake until cooked.

Method of Icing Cake

When icing a large cake covered with marzipan, ice the top first and leave this to harden for perhaps about a day. Do the sides next and repeat this process if giving a second coat – by this method you avoid smudging the sides. When you have covered the cake, design your decoration taking into consideration any flaws in the icing. To plan a design for the cake, cut out a piece of greaseproof paper exactly the size of the top of the cake and on this paper work out your design. When you have finished the design, place the piece of paper on top of the cake and, with a large pin, outline the decoration with little pin pricks.

Royal Icing

Ingredients
900g (2 lbs) icing sugar
4 whites of egg
A little glycerine
Colouring, if desired.

Method

Whisk egg whites lightly and gradually add in sieved icing sugar. When you have some of this mixed in, add a little glycerine. This is to stop the icing from going very hard if it is left for any length of time. When colouring icing, add colouring very very slowly.

Christmas Cake

Ingredients
One 20cm (8 in) round fruit cake
900g (2 lbs) marzipan
Apricot jam
900g (2 lbs) icing, 9/10ths white, 1/10th red

Method

Cover with marzipan as directed, and then cover with two layers of white icing. Work out design for top of cake by using greaseproof paper the exact size of the cake and trace this onto the cake. The star is done with a No. 5 star pipe. Place the cake on a cake board and finish the base with icing and then place the ribbon on it as in photograph. Place decorations in centre. Pipes used are No. 14 star pipe for stars and No. 12 pipe for base.

Golden Wedding Cake

Ingredients
One 20cm (8 in) round fruit cake
900g (2 lbs) marzipan
Jam
900g (2 lbs) yellow coloured icing

Method

Cover cake with marzipan as already described and then give it two coats of icing. Work out design on a piece of paper. Carry out decoration as carefully as possible and place whatever type Golden Wedding decorations which you desire. Follow design as in photograph. All design on this cake was done with a No. 10 pipe and the writing was done with an icing pen.

Christening Cake

Ingredients
One 18cm (7 in) square fruit cake
900g (2 lbs) marzipan
Apricot jam
Pink royal icing
20cm (8 in) square cake board
Two different widths of pink ribbon, (one dark colour and one light colour)
Christening decoration

Method

Cover cake with marzipan and then give it two coats of pink royal icing. Decoration is done with a stronger pink, trace out your decoration on a piece of greaseproof paper exactly the size of the top of the cake and draw out the design which you require. Follow the design in the photograph and put ribbons and cradle in place. The designs were done by No. 2 plain pipe for trellis, No. 14 pipe for stars and No. 12 pipe for base. The writing is done with an icing pen.

1933
1983
50
SEONA
ELIZABETH
21·2·83

Step by Step Cookery

Basic White Sauce

Ingredients
25g (1 oz) flour
25g (1 oz) Scottish butter
280ml ($\frac{1}{2}$ pint) milk
Seasoning

Method

1. Melt butter in pan.
   Blend in flour to make a roux.

2. Cook roux for one minute, stirring.

3. Gradually blend in milk.

4. Return to heat and bring to boil stirring all the time. Cook for 2-3 minutes. Season.

Macaroni Cheese

Ingredients
50g (2 oz) macaroni
280ml ($\frac{1}{2}$ pint) white sauce
75g (3 oz) Scottish cheddar cheese, grated
Little mustard

Method

1. Boil macaroni for 12 minutes and drain.

2. Add cheese and mustard to sauce and stir.

3. Add macaroni and stir well.

4. Place in ovenproof dish and grill, if desired, with cheese on top.

Egg Custard

Oven temperature: 150°C/300°F/ No. 2
Position in oven: Middle
Time in oven: 45 minutes-1 hour

Ingredients
2 egg yolks
3 eggs
50g (2 oz) sugar
560ml (1 pint) milk, heated to blood temperature
Little nutmeg

Method

1. Lightly whisk all eggs and sugar. Whisk in milk.
2. Pour through a sieve into a greased ovenproof dish.

3. Shake a little nutmeg on top. Place in a roasting tin containing enough water to come about halfway up the sides of the dish.
4. Bake until set.

Crème Caramel

Make up egg custard to Stage 2.
Add ½ teaspoon vanilla essence.

Caramel Ingredients
2 tablespoons water
50g (2 oz) sugar

Method

1. Place water and sugar in a thick pan and heat to caramel colour.

2. Pour caramel into greased dariole moulds.

3. Pour custard mixture on top. Cook in oven as Stage 3 of egg custard but without nutmeg.

4. Turn out onto a serving dish. Serve hot or cold with cream.

Shortcrust Pastry

Oven temperature: 190°C/375°F/ No. 5
Position in oven: Centre
Time in oven: 15-20 minutes

Ingredients
100g (4 oz) plain flour
$\frac{1}{4}$ level teaspoon salt
50g (2 oz) Scottish butter (cut in small pieces)
Cold water to mix

Method

1. Sieve flour and salt into bowl. Add butter and rub into flour with fingertips.

2. Add water and mix in with a round bladed knife.

3. Turn out onto a floured board, knead gently and roll out.

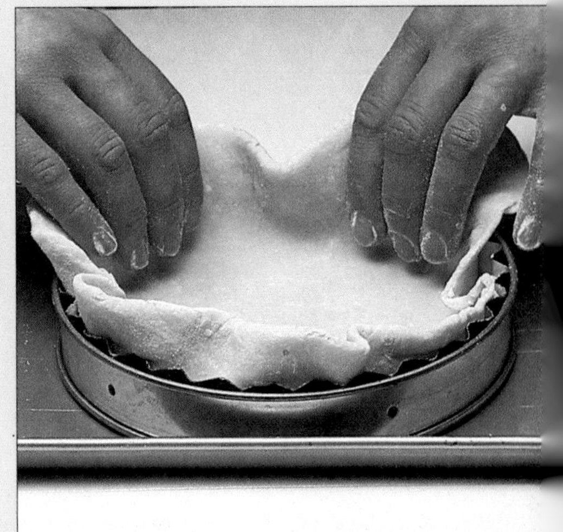

4. Line flan ring with pastry. Prick base and bake blind*.

*Bake pastry with no filling. To do this, crumple up some tinfoil and place round edge of flan to stop sides falling in. Remove after half the cooking time.

Fudge Meringue Flan

Oven temperature: 150°C/300°F/ No. 2
Position in oven: Centre
Time in oven: 20-30 minutes

Ingredients

1 × 397g (14 oz) tin of condensed milk, boiled for 2 hours in tin, then cooled
2 egg whites
100g (4 oz) caster sugar

Method

1. Open tin and empty into flan case.

2. Whisk up egg whites till stiff then fold in sugar.

3. Pipe or fork meringue on top of filling.

4. Bake in oven until meringue is golden brown.

Basic Batter

Ingredients
100g (4 oz) flour, sieved
1 egg
280ml ($\frac{1}{2}$ pint) milk
Seasoning

Method

1. Sieve flour and salt.

2. Add egg and a little milk.

3. Beat well.

4. Gradually add remainder of milk. Leave for $\frac{1}{2}$ hour.

Lemon Pancakes

Ingredients

Batter (see page 120)
Scottish butter
Lemon juice
Caster sugar

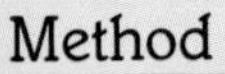
Method

1. Pour a little batter into a hot frying pan brushed with melted butter.

2. When batter is set and underside brown, turn and brown second side.

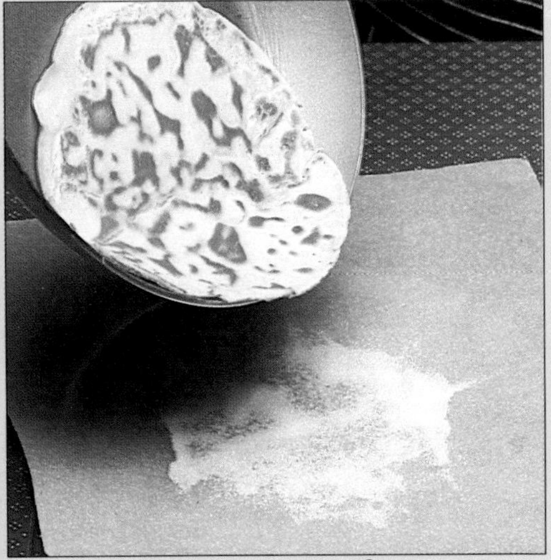

3. Turn onto greaseproof paper with sugar on it. Squeeze lemon juice on top and fold pancake over.

4. Keep hot in a warm oven until all pancakes are ready.

Butter Sponge

Oven temperature: 190°C/375°F/ No. 5
Position in oven: Centre
Time in oven: 25 minutes

Ingredients
100g (4 oz) Scottish butter
100g (4 oz) caster sugar
150g (6 oz) self-raising flour, sieved
2 eggs, beaten
1-2 dessertspoons hot water

Method
1. Cream butter and sugar thoroughly by hand or mixer.

2. Add eggs and flour alternately.

3. Add hot water to form soft dropping consistency and place in two 18cm (7 in) buttered tins.

4. Bake in oven until top is golden brown and cake has shrunk slightly away from sides of tins. When cool sandwich together with jam or lemon curd and dust with icing sugar.

Egg Sponge

Oven temperature: 220°C/425°F/ No. 7
Position in oven: Top half
Time in oven: 10 minutes

Ingredients
100g (4 oz) self-raising flour, sieved
4 eggs
100g (4 oz) caster sugar
Filling:
140ml ($\frac{1}{4}$ pint) whipping cream
Jam
Little caster sugar

Method
1. Whisk eggs and sugar together until creamy with whisk or mixer.

2. Carefully fold in flour.

3. Pour mixture into two 18cm (7 in) buttered tins.

4. Bake in oven till firm and set. Place on cooling tray.
When cold, spread with jam, then whipped cream. Dust with caster sugar.

Index